THE TODDLER GUIDE
FOR DADS

ESSENTIAL TIPS ON DISCIPLINE, POTTY TRAINING, AND PARENTING FOR A FIRST-TIME FATHER

JOHN NERO

CONTENTS

information contained within this document, including, but not limited to, errors, omissions, or inaccuracies.

Just for you

A FREE GIFT TO MY READERS

Learn 7 tips that will help you build an incredible
bond with your baby, just visit

www.johnnero.com

and click free books

INTRODUCTION

"A father carries pictures where his money used to be." — Steve Martin

New parents are bombarded with differing information regarding even the basics of how to raise their children. There's a sea of it all over the web, and some of it is conflicting information! Not to mention, most of it rarely focuses on the father as the primary caregiver. Unfortunately, fathers are often left out of the parenting discussion, both professionally and socially.

In today's society, fathers are becoming more and more integral in the act of caregiving. While fathers were not expected to be primary caregivers, the tides have changed in the last few decades! As most of the research surrounding parenting focuses on the mother as the primary caregiver, this book exists to give tips, tricks, and education to fathers.

Despite the fact that the role of the father is changing to become more nurturing and emotionally involved, fathers aren't supplied with information specifically tailored to them.

This probably isn't news to you at all. You're experiencing it after all. You're a new father and all the information your doctors may be telling you are things they expect you to relay to your partner or to the child's mother, rather than teaching you specifically. You were never given the information about how to parent, what styles of parenting are best for your child's development — or even what child development even is!

And none of this is your fault. As a man in this society, you probably lack realistic role models or expectations when it comes to fatherhood. The engaged father is a new concept, a revolution in the realm of parenting. You were likely expected instead to be the family breadwinner, to prioritize work (and thus you were likely never given paid leave!).

Dads, this is your ultimate guide. Whether you're the primary caregiver or not, there are going to be times when you need to get involved. In order to capitalize on the key moments of your child's life and create strong relationships and trust with your children, as well as learn how to care for them in the earliest stages of their life, you should know all the information in the following pages.

The first thing you need to know is this — what it takes to be a good father. Since you picked up this book, you're likely already well on your way. The fathers you watched in your favorite sitcoms are probably not the type of dads you should aspire to, so instead, let me tell you this: a good father engages.

Being a dad takes a lifetime of patience and all the love you have to give in your heart. Your child should be the focus of your life, just as much as you're going to be the focus of your child's life — especially during these formative years as your infant becomes a toddler. As your child develops cognitively, they will begin forming strong attachments to their parents. You want to ensure that your child is securely attached to you and your partner, and to do this, you need to be there.

Showing up is half the battle with parenting. Living with your kids, taking time out of your day to attend important events, and spending time with your tots have a positive impact on your child. There are tons of literature in this regard in the psychology community that shows that an active father that participates in caregiving and household chores impacts the child's cognitive development profoundly — in a good way. Showing up, however, doesn't mean just being in the room. It means connecting with your child and your partner as much as you can.

It goes without saying that there are significant emotional, social, and behavioral benefits linked to having a father in the picture in early childhood, especially active fathers that are deeply involved with their children's care. Infants attain higher cognitive scores at age one if their fathers were involved in their lives throughout infancy. The benefits last all throughout childhood, with better scores in schools and at work well into the future.

High-quality, engaged parenting starts from birth. It remains especially important during the formative years of toddlerhood well into childhood and the (perhaps dreaded) teenage years. But you already knew that! Your commitment to raising your child in the best way possible will carry you through these years. As your child begins to develop a personality of their own, you'll start to have a lot more fun with your kids — you'll be able to bond in a much more dynamic way with your toddler than you could when they were an infant.

With that being said, there are going to be some rough times too. At this stage, you should prepare yourself for the behavioral changes of your child, which can at times be rocky to say the least. Your efforts, however, matter so much more than you realize. As fathers, it's important to be the embodiment of good qualities and virtues so that we can be good role models to our children. That doesn't mean that you have to be perfect — you're human, and expecting perfection is unrealistic. However, it does mean that you'll have to learn how to navigate your mistakes healthily in ways that your child can learn from. How you treat yourself directly influences how your child will grow to treat themselves!

For your convenience, this book is structured so as to give you the general information you need to know from year to year. This includes developmental milestones! From there, we go into the specifics of your tot's needs during those years. We will also be discussing parenting methods and how to keep your little one safe throughout their early childhood.

So, dads, buckle up. Your child isn't the only one who's going through a transformative period in their lifetime. As you raise your child, you will realize just all that you are capable of — things you probably never expected you could do. Embrace the changes that are about to come your way and let this experience turn you into the man you want to be for your child's sake. Without any further ado, let's get into the basics of raising a toddler!

TODDLER BASICS

*A*fter the first year of your baby's life, your child will become a toddler. It's around this time that your baby has started to be able to sit on their own without support. They may even be able to stand on their own or walk with the help of something to hold on to. This is actually where the word "toddler" comes from — to toddle is to walk with short, uncertain steps.

The beginnings of independence find their roots in this stage of development. It's only been a year, and that may seem too fast for you, but don't worry. Your child knows, biologically, when it's the appropriate time for them to explore the world around them in their own ways. You'll still need to watch over them, of course. Their bodies may know it's time, but their minds certainly don't understand the dangers of their environment.

The toddler stage lasts for about two years. The end of toddlerhood is characterized by your child's ability to walk, talk, feed and do simple tasks for themselves. In the meantime, you're going to need to know how to properly foster those skills!

In this chapter, we'll be covering the absolute basics of toddler care. In this transformative stage, your child will be highly impressionable, and it is key that you nourish your child's development as much as possible. To do this, you need to understand the fundamental needs of your toddler.

While reading through the following advice, ensure that you are also checking back with your pediatrician regarding your tot's needs. Every child is different, so regularly checking up with your child's doctors will give you your best idea about how your child operates.

When it comes to nutrition, clothing, play, and other developmental tools, there are some golden rules and guidelines to follow and understand! This chapter covers all of the above.

EATING AND NUTRITION

Good nutrition during the first two years of life is crucial for healthy growth and development. Starting with healthy nutrition practices early in life can set the stage for great eating behavior and attitudes for the rest of your child's life.

Most 1- to 3-year-olds thrive on three meals and two to three snacks a day. Toddlers have a lot of energy and small stomachs, which means they'll be eating more frequently than you will. Albeit, in much smaller quantities.

In order to keep a handle on your child's diet, you'll need a good structure. Plan on offering snacks at regular times instead of on-demand. Weaving your snack times between your meal times is a good plan to keep your tot on a consistent eating schedule, which they will eventually grow used to. This helps establish a circadian rhythm with your child — that is, healthy sleeping routines. We'll discuss this more later on.

The key with meals and snacks is being consistent. Consistent schedules aids in keeping your tot from getting crabby and over-hungry. It will also help keep your tot from asking for food all the time.

Toddler years are transitory years, especially between 1-2 years of age. Toddlers spend this time learning to eat table food, accepting new tastes and textures (and thoroughly rejecting the ones they don't like).

Your toddler may not eat the same amount every day. Your little one will eat according to their hunger or fullness, but it is important to try and encourage your kids to eat even the foods they don't like.

You should also be prepared for the fact that on some days food will get eaten and on other days food may decorate your floor and walls. Your child knows when they're hungry enough to eat, so allow them some leeway with their diet. Encourage them, but do not force-feed your child.

There are different daily allotments between two-year-old tots and three-year-old tots, this is because your child is entering a new stage of development that incorporates more physical growth spurts.

The average daily food amounts for two-year-olds:

- Grains - 3 ounces
- Vegetables - 1 cup
- Fruits - 1 cup

- Milk - 2 cups
- Meat and beans - 2 ounces

The average daily food amounts for three-year-olds:

- Grains - 4-5 ounces
- Vegetables - 1 ½ cups
- Fruits - 1-1 ½ cups
- Milk - 2 cups
- Meat and beans - 3-4 ounces

Milk is extremely important for its calcium levels, and iron-rich meats are important as well. While these are important for growth, you want to limit the intake of both. Too much calcium may put your tot at risk for an iron deficiency, so you want to stay within the guidelines.

It's important to offer your toddler three regular meals and healthy snacks. While growth has slowed since your child's infancy stage, so your child no longer eats as much as they used to. However, your tot's brain and muscles still need a lot of energy as they develop in these years, so be sure to be consistent with your feeding schedule.

Sample Feeding Schedule

In this sample, please keep in mind that this is suited for the average toddler. If your tot does better on a schedule that doesn't look exactly like that below, that's perfectly fine as well. Everyone is different, and no two toddlers are created equally! You should make sure that you consult your pediatrician for advice regarding your tot's diet, especially if there are any dietary restrictions to keep in mind.

- 8:00 am: Wake up! With any luck, your tot will be able to sleep until this point!
- 8:30 am: Make some breakfast! Please do note, if you make a habit of eating with your tot at this time, that it does help reinforce the habit, and keeping on the schedule will become easier for your little one.
- 10:00 am or 10:30 am: Depending on how breakfast goes, and how hungry your tot is, a small snack before lunch will be called for. Remember, let your toddler dictate their food intake!
- 12:30 pm: Lunchtime! As with breakfast, you'll want to be eating with your toddler to establish that habit with them.
- 1:30 pm: Lay your tot down for a nap, and

try to get one in yourself if you can! Naps aren't just for the kiddos, after all.

- 3:30 pm: Now it's time for an afternoon snack. Your toddler may or may not be hungry at this point due to the nap, so just keep this in mind. You may want to nudge this earlier in the day by an hour so that your toddler will be tired by bedtime.

- 5:30 pm: Time for dinner! Hopefully, you and your partner will be able to eat together with your tot. Creating a schedule of having dinner together is not only good for scheduled maintenance, but especially for family bonding.

- 8:00 pm: Now, it's time for your tot to go to bed. Lay them down for the night, and catch some rest yourself when you can!

Dads, it's important to keep in mind that your child needs to see you participating in the act of caring and cleaning. Better yet, do those things together with your tot. Toddlers are incredibly impressionable! When you make snacks with your toddler and clean the home with your toddler around, this will have beneficial cognitive effects in the long run.

Toddler-Friendly Snacks

None of the foods you offer should have much sugar or salt. Preferably, the snacks you give would have none! Children require foods that are high in healthy fats, like salmon and avocado.

That being said, you're going to want to be able to offer your tots a wide variety of foods. It's important for the development of your child's palate, and for the sake of discouraging pickiness when it comes to food, to have your child exposed to many different types of textures and tastes in their foods.

Here are some ideas for snacks that you can safely give your tot between meals:

- oatmeal or whole-grain cereal (you can add milk if you like)
- cooked beef, chicken, or tofu (bite-sized!) and soft-cooked vegetables
- milk or yogurt-based smoothies
- apple sauce with whole-grain crackers
- fresh fruits
- yogurt or fruit popsicles
- pita bread triangles and bean dips
- small cubes of cheese, or grated cheese, with crackers

If you're lucky enough to have a toddler that enjoys vegetables, you can offer those as much as you like.

WALKING AND GOOD SHOES

Your toddler's feet aren't yet fully developed, so they need to be protected. Toddlers are flat-footed when they start walking. Their bones, muscles, and ligaments aren't strong enough to support an arch. While pediatricians recommend that your child goes without footwear as often as possible to encourage your tot's balance, posture, and coordination, there are simply times when barefoot isn't feasible.

There's a broad average between when your child will first begin to walk. Anywhere from eight months to eighteen months of age is the timeframe most children tend to fall in while taking their first steps.

At home, ensure that your floor is clean so that your toddler isn't in danger while they explore their world upright for the first time. In the beginning stages, try to keep your tot barefoot as they experiment. They will be using the soles of their feet to feel the ground beneath them and develop their muscle strength!

After you've given your tot some time to walk around, and they seem much more confident, that's when you will want to advance into wearing shoes.

How to Pick a Good Shoe

The growth of a children's foot is a bit of a nightmare to navigate. Like most growth spurts, they tend to come on strong and taper off after a little bit of time. Between the ages one to four, your child will experience many growth spurts in the foot as their bodies prepare to grow taller.

Because of this frequency of growth, you'll want to stay on top of measuring your children's feet on a regular basis. Monthly or bimonthly is a good timeframe for measurement, as you'll be able to pick up on the trends of your children's growth spurts and prepare for the future.

You might be tempted to go with your most expensive options. We've been trained to believe that expensive means quality in our society, though this is not always the case. Your tot will have specific needs when it comes to their shoes — perhaps medical needs. Though toddlers tend to be flat-footed, your pediatrician will be able to discern whether or not your children's arches are developing at a healthy rate and whether their feet are tilting in or out. Ensure that you seek the advice of your pediatrician, if that is the case. You may need to look at shoes with more arch support, or have custom sole inserts made to support your children's legs and hips.

Getting proper shoes is incredibly important to the lasting health of your child's foot arches, hips, and spine. In order to measure your children's shoes, you can do the following:

1. Stand your child up against a wall. You want your tot to be standing straight with their back touching the wall, but not leaning so that their weight is equally distributed between their feet.

2. Ensure that your children's heels touch the wall. This is just so you have an easy-to-see zero point to measure from. This could easily be a book or even a straight line drawn on the floor if that's easier.

3. From the wall (or whatever it is you used), measure your tot's foot with a ruler (or a tape measure). You'll want to measure the distance between the wall and the tip of their longest toe. This is usually the big toe, but

can also be the toe directly beside the big toe.

4. If your child's longest toe is not the big toe, this may have an effect on the type of shoe you need to buy for your child. Some shoes have steeper tapers towards the end of the shoes, so ensure you get a shoe with a shallow taper, so it doesn't squeeze your child's toes. Some stores will sell a wide shoe size variation, which could be an option for you.

5. Press your thumb against the end of the shoe with your child's foot inside. If you feel your child's toe pressed right to the edge of the material, then you know the shoe's shape isn't right for your child.

6. Ensure that you are taking your measurements in the metric your country uses to size shoes. The metric system tends to be most commonly used when looking at shoe sizes online.

Something to keep in mind while you're measuring your children's foot is that the height and width of the shoe are also important. While a shoe should be snug, your child's foot should never be pressed tight against the material of the shoe. Rather, the shoe should be fastened to be tight to the foot rather than tight-fitting to begin with.

To navigate shoe sizes, you'll want to try a bunch of different shoes. If you're concerned with the width of the shoes in question, a good way to go about figuring out how wide your tot's foot is is to print off a sheet with the size border. You can find a bunch of these online, but shoe stores also have special measurement devices that can accurately size your tot's feet. Your pediatrician will also have access to tools like this, so if you ever have any questions, you can consult with them as well.

Your tot's foot should fall within the borders of the print-outs, if you decide to use those. If you're measuring yourself, make sure to keep in mind that the inside of the shoe will measure differently than the outside. This is because of the materials of the shoe. You'll want to take the measurement of the inside sole, not the full shoe itself, to account for the difference in thickness of the materials used in the shoe.

Though it's never a bad thing to want your children to look good, ensure that you're not going with trends that could cause unhealthy development in your children's feet. For example, Converse are certainly cool-looking and trendy, but that's all they are. Trendy shoes, on average, don't account for the needs of a toddler's delicate, developing bone structure. Going with shoes without ensuring that the shoes are tailored for toddlers can result in a slew of medical issues down the line, ranging anywhere from spinal issues like scoliosis or pigeon toes. These conditions are treatable, but it's better to avoid the danger altogether and just get a shoe you know will support your child's health.

Your child will begin to develop their own styles, too. At one, it's likely your tot will just be happy with whatever it is you end up picking. At four, though, you may never hear the end of it if you get the wrong shoe!

To navigate this, you should go with your tot to a store that specializes in toddler's shoes. You can get an accurate measurement there, and ensure that the shoes you buy are going to be good quality and made for their needs. This will also allow your child some say in the process of buying the shoe! They'll love their shoes more if they get to pick the ones they like. You may even have a hard time getting them out of their shoes when you get back home!

Teaching Your Child How to Dress Themselves

As they say, "Monkey see, monkey do." When it comes to teaching your child how to dress themselves, this rule is king.

While you're teaching your child to dress themselves, allow them to be in the same room with you as you get dressed. Or better yet, get dressed together. Your toddler will be able to see your example as you explain what you're doing — and you'll need to explain everything to your tot.

You'll want to start teaching with large clothing first. That way, your child can differentiate the orientation of the clothing better.

Regarding zippers, you'll want to be careful to teach your tot how to steer clear of getting their skin caught in them. Zipping is a complicated skill, however, so you should not expect them to be doing this themselves. The fine motor skills required for zipping won't be fully mastered until your child is about five or six. Meanwhile, teach them how to lock a zipper into its track by allowing them to watch you, and zip it up yourself. As time goes on, you can guide your tots hands along with these actions so that they are physically doing it themselves with you. The skill will eventually become mastered through this process.

The same goes for buttons. The act of slipping a button through a tiny hole requires much more fine motor skills than your child is capable of for the first few years of their lives, so expect that this will be slow as well. Until then, make sure they watch you do this for them. Explain what you do at the same time, and eventually, your tot will grasp it.

As an alternative to buttons or zippers, snaps are likely the easiest option to teach your child how to fasten clothes to themselves. Your child may be shaky at first learning how to handle a snap and press down on it with enough pressure for the snap to lock, but after some strength develops in those tiny fingers, they'll get the hang of it!

Be careful as you slip on your child's shoes. When you teach them how to do this for themselves, make sure that any laces or straps are undone. Make sure you watch your child to ensure that they do not accidentally fold the shoe underneath their heel — and show them how to fix it if they do. When the shoe is on your child's foot, show them how to strap their straps! Knot tying can be shown, but your child will likely not be able to do this for quite a bit of time.

With pants, make sure you teach your child to sit down while they're putting pants on for the time being. You can guide one foot into each leg individually, and then show your child how to shimmy them up themselves by doing it for them and letting them watch you do it for yourself.

Much like pants, jackets should be taught with one sleeve at a time. Until your child is at the age where they can zip up their own jackets, you'll need to be the one zipping it up for them. However, since jackets are usually rather large, children get a handle of putting them on faster than most other clothes.

A bit trickier is the pullover tops, like t-shirts and long sleeved shirts. You'll want to teach your child to put their head through the head hole first, rolling up the shirt so that they don't get lost in it in the meantime. When their head is through, then teach them how to stretch the shirt to put one arm through the sleeve at a time. Your tot should be able to master this more quickly than they can do zippers or buttons, but don't be concerned if it takes longer than you feel it should. Your toddler will learn at their own pace.

PLAYTIME

While play is incredibly important throughout a person's entire lifetime, play is especially important as your child's cognitive and somatic functions begin to develop. In truth, play is how toddlers learn how to use their bodies — the limitations they have, how to control their strength, and so on. Play also encourages the development of your child's creativity, problem-solving abilities, and emotional strength.

Your toddler's very first interaction with the world will be through play. When your child seeks to understand the functions around them, you'll notice they drift into play that revolves around the imaginary. This is good — they are interacting with the world in ways that they can control, which will aid them in developing understanding of their environment in conjunction with conquering their fear of the unknown. This is because children who are confident in their environments will carry this through to other environments.

Aside from emotional maturation, your child's education depends on play. Your child will be most engaged when they are playing — a fact that is being utilized more and more in elementary schools today. Making a game of learning, or allowing your children to make games that use the content to be learned, is a great way to keep your toddler interested in new ideas. This advice can be carried all throughout your child's development, too.

There are also benefits play has on your tot's physical development. Hands-on games, or other multi-sensory exercises, stimulate your toddler's brain. This helps them hone their critical thinking skills, as well as their motor skills. Playing games with puzzles, for instance, has your child use their problem-solving brain in tandem with their eyes and cognitive ability to distinguish shapes and distance. All of this has beneficial effects on your child's brain development, specifically in areas that govern analytical and geometric skills, such as the right parietal lobe.

Play that involves moving their body also helps your child develop strength in their limbs. For example, your baby might love to push off the ground in their baby bouncer, jumping all around. This is excellent for cultivating the strength in your child's legs. Additionally, any play that makes them get up on their feet will help them learn how to balance and move around bi-pedally.

We will discuss more in later chapters how to encourage play in ways that best benefit your child. For now, your child's playtime will be influenced by you! Children need to learn to play as much as they need to learn from playing. They will take cues from you during the first months of their lifetime. You can use this to bond with your child, by keeping them active alongside you wherever your play leads you.

How to Help Your Toddler Make Friends

Admittedly, toddlers aren't well-known for their social skills. Even among their peers, toddlers may have difficulties with making friends. They can't exactly strike up a conversation with someone their own size, especially if they're barely past infancy!

You can help your toddler make friends by introducing them to a small group of children — perhaps even just a one-on-one play date supervised by yourself and another parent. It might be tempting to have a big gathering, but you should absolutely avoid this. Too many children at a time can be very overwhelming to a toddler, even if they do seem to have good social graces.

Perhaps one of your friends has a child. The two of you could organize a playdate, or a small outing with both of your kids. Not only will this be good for your child's socialization, but it'll be good for *yours* as well, Dad. You probably haven't seen your friends in a while!

If none of your friends has children, make new ones. You can find groups for parents in all manners of spots on the internet. There could also be events catered to parents with small children where you can meet people. Through this, you may even notice that there's another tot your child tends to gravitate to. You should try to befriend that child's caregivers, so the two can play together!

The Best Toys For Tots

While you can get away with a ton of different types of toys, the ones that are best for your child are those that require the use of more than one of their skills. Before we get into this, a note: your child's toys are not, and should not be, gendered. If your little boy wants to play with dolls, there is nothing wrong with that. If your little girl loves monster truck toys, that's great, too. They're both healthy toys for your child's development, gender is irrelevant. Here is a list of ideas for good toys:

- Puzzles
- Push-Pull Toys (especially ones that make your child stand up!)
- Ride-On Toys
- Balls
- Stuffed Animals and Dolls
- Blocks and Building Systems
- Vehicles
- Dollhouses and Play Sets

DEVELOPMENT

By now, you've heard the word "development" several times. You may be wondering what it means and what all it entails. The answer to these questions is, well, everything that has to do with your child's life.

When one says development as they're discussing children, they're talking about the sequential processes that play into language, physical, emotional, and cognitive skills. Development is most commonly used for children, as children go through most of the stages of development rather quickly, and they are the most studied aspect of development within psychology. However, development is a lifetime endeavor. Even you are still in the process of development!

In this book, we will be discussing development as it pertains to the milestones your child will experience in every year leading up to childhood. There will be much to cover, and it will be discussed at the beginning of every chapter.

For now, though, understand that your toddler's erratic behaviors are due to the fact that your child simply hasn't reached a developmental milestone that allows them to self-govern and impulse control. This comes much later, in fact. You can expect your tot to swing drastically from assertive to shy, aggressive to gentle, independent to clingy, loud to lethargic, and so on. This will probably cause some headaches — it can sometimes even feel like you're living with a stranger.

As fathers, it's important that you don't see this as good or bad. Rather, all the behaviors your child exhibits should be considered teachable moments for the both of you. Bonding moments, most importantly. Your child is too young to understand the concepts of "good" and "bad;" they're not doing the things they're doing out of any malicious or benevolent intention. Rather, these are concepts you instill in your child based on how you react to their behavior — so make sure you react with patience and a fair attitude.

It can often be frustrating to teach right from wrong, self-control, and how to give respect to others (even if they're strangers). You'll likely be spending a lot of time with your tot to tell them that a behavior they did was wrong and explaining that to them. As your child develops, understand that you should never react to their behavior angrily. Your ability to reason with your child and be sensitive to their emotional state is your best way to deal with unwanted behavior.

There are going to be some messy times, so make sure you take some time to recharge when you can. Leaning on your partner to help with the disciplinary portion of care will make this process easier. You can also lean on your near family and friends. Your child will respond to all of you as adults and will look to each of you for direction on how to behave, so it's important that all of you act together and present a unified front to your toddler to weed out unwanted behavior. As they say, it takes a village to raise a child.

First Steps

At around eight months of age, your child is standing. Or, they're working on standing. From there, your baby's first steps might happen within a few days or a few months of when they first learn to stand.

Children will start trying to learn to take their first steps slowly. They'll graduate from standing for short periods of time to pulling themselves upright for longer periods of time. Around nine to twelve months, you may even notice your child clutching to the surfaces of furniture and inching along that way.

It will usually take your child between eleven and thirteen months to be walking around independently. However, this can take longer. Your child may be anxious to start walking, despite being physically able to do so. The reason for this is that children know that they're wobbly, and are cautious when it comes to moving around upright (especially if they've tumbled before). Gently encourage your child by guiding them with their hands as they learn to walk, so they can build their confidence in their walking skills.

If your child is a daredevil, they may jump right in and not need your support at all. Kids are all unique! Allow your child to dictate their own pace, and they'll reach those milestones with your support.

Tips to Encourage Good Cognitive and Physical Development

There are ways you can support your child through their development which will have lasting benefits to your child as they grow. Some of these activities will have immediate benefits to helping your child past a milestone, while others may leave lasting impressions on your child that helps them develop healthy habits. One example of the latter is reading.

It's important to read to your toddler daily. Reading helps children develop their vocabularies and understanding of their language. It will also help them understand how books function — a useful skill for when they get to a schooling age that your teachers will thank you for! Reading before bedtime is also a great way to help relax your child.

Quiz your toddler by asking them to find objects for you or to name body parts and objects. Your child is developing their understanding of the world around them. While they may not get everything correctly, they can learn from their mistakes this way. You can teach them what the objects are that they bring to you, if they're not the correct ones.

You should encourage your child to explore and solve small problems for themselves. Don't try to solve everything for your child all the time. Support your child by giving hints to them on how to solve those problems, and allow them to work it out for themselves! You can do this easily with matching games, shape sorting games, or other simple puzzles.

Speaking of exploration, you should also encourage curiosity, and take frequent trips to the park or going on bus rides. Allow your child to wander with you and take in the sights of the environment they grow up in.

Another thing you should do often is talk with your toddler. If you're not good at baby voice, which admittedly many of us dads may struggle with, there's nothing wrong with that. Studies suggest that speaking normally with your child helps them develop their language skills quickly. To help them learn new words, you can enunciate the words for things you think they're saying — for instance, if your tot says "baba," you can say instead that it is a "bottle."

Speaking with your tot ties into discipline as well. Respond to wanted behaviors more than you punish unwanted behaviors. Always use reason with your toddler, by showing or telling them what they should do instead. Never yell at your child. Remember, how you react to your tot at these early ages will dictate how they react to the world around them in the future. If you treat your child with patient kindness even when they're doing something wrong, they will grow up healthier for it and with a better perspective of the world.

When your tot is to the point of wanting to help dress themselves, allow them to do so! Your toddler may reach to try and do the snaps or buttons themselves. As soon as they show an interest in helping with these types of actions, let them.

POTTY TRAINING

Where it comes to potty training, there are many misconceptions, which lead parents down the wrong paths. Let's discuss a few of them.

One, that there's no perfect time to potty-train. There's no catch-all for kids, and the average timeframe of 18-36 months is a generalization that your kid may not fall into (especially if your toddler is a boy). There's nothing wrong with that.

Another myth rolling around parental hemispheres is that disposable pull-on diapers interfere with the act of potty training. This has never been proven and is not the case. Pull-on diapers help you keep your house and your child's clothes from getting messy. They're considered a good middle step when it comes to potty training! Your toddler can experience a full range of independence while retaining the security a diaper provides.

Something else we should clear up: boys are not harder to train than girls. When your child is ready to be trained, they will be more receptive to learning regardless of their gender. With that said, boys and girls do have different needs in regard to potty training — different equipment begets different methods of approach, after all. Regarding the potty.

Additionally, daycares will not take care of potty training for you. Early childhood educators (ECEs) aren't a replacement for potty training your child yourself, and often they will have more children to juggle their attention between, so they wouldn't be able to commit as much energy to training your toddler as may be needed. However, early childhood educators are willing to work with parents. If you communicate with your ECEs, they can ensure that what's happening at home is what happens at daycare.

This even includes when your child is using their equipment. You may be wondering what kinds of things you'll want to have on hand during the potty-training process — it's no simpler than a potty. However, not all potties are created equally. Your potty needs to have space for your child to lean forward with their feet on the ground while in a sitting position, especially when your child is having a bowel movement. You'll also want to ensure that your potties are secure and don't rock around when your child is using them.

Don't be tempted to skip the potty step and go straight to the toilet step. There's a lot of anxiety surrounding the toilet for your child. Toilets are large for the tot! They are at risk of falling into, or off of, the toilet — and this worry can interfere with the training. If you absolutely have to skip the potty step for any reason, ensure that you install an adapter seat on your toilet. It should be secure and comfortable. You'll also need a stool so that your child can easily get on and off, as well as stabilize their feet while they go.

At the end of the day, it's not uncommon that parents say that this is their least favorite milestone. However, it's important not to see it for the potentially huge stinky messes it can sometimes come with. Potty training is core to the development of your child's confidence and independence. The training itself is what you make it to be. If you make it a fun time with your tot, both you and your child will have a better, healthier experience.

Signs My Toddler May be Ready to be Potty Trained

Timing is the key to successful potty training. You can't force potty training on a child who isn't ready, as it will only prolong the process. There's no universal rule for when your child will be ready to start potty training, but there are some signs that you can pick up on to gauge your child's readiness. For example:

- Your child may exhibit interest in the toilet, potty, or even in underpants. If you're pretty open with your bathroom habits, it's likely your child is trying to figure out what you're doing on the pot!
- You're changing fewer wet diapers. You may notice that your kid is staying dry for two or more hours, even.
- They're pooping on predictable schedules!
- They broadcast their bodily functions. Your tot may tell you what they're doing right as they're doing it (hopefully in a diaper), but further on into the process, you'll notice that your child may be holding it in. They may even tell you when they need to go, using verbal cues like grunting or body language cues like crossing their legs, maybe even going into a corner.

- They despise wet or dirty diapers, and want to be changed as soon as they can.
- Your child should also exhibit readiness by understanding the language of the potty, like "pee" and "poop."

Your child must be able to follow simple instructions, both mentally and physically. It's important that you be able to tell your child what to do, and that they can do those tasks for themselves. For instance, you'll want your child to be able to pull their own pants up and down. They should also be able to sit down and get up from a potty chair all on their own.

The Mindset and the Set-Up

If you believe your child is ready to be potty-trained, and you're ready to do the training, it's time to clear your calendar. You're going to need some good one-on-one time during the process, as this will help your child learn faster. Be sure not to rush, however. Let the process be a bonding moment for you and your child, and when they're done, you can worry about having the potty party.

You'll need to have all your equipment ready to start. Your adapter seats should be installed, or your potties placed strategically in your bathrooms that are easily accessible from your toddler's usual living spaces. Some parents may even choose to have potties in every main room as well as in the bathroom to start with. The latter is a great way to keep really on top of the process, especially if your child doesn't give you much warning before they're popping a squat over your carpet. If you see a sign, then you can quickly get your child onto the nearest potty without having to go too far to start.

If you have any toys, books, or rewards for the process, these will also be helpful to you and your tot. Books can be especially helpful to you, if they have illustrations of the act of potty training. They'll help you explain to your child what the potty is.

Rewards are also great behavior reinforcers. If you show your children rewards for using the potty, their brain wires that as being a good thing to do! Repetition and consistent rewards for good behavior with the potty is necessary for the early stages, and helps make the training stick. An example of a reward you could give are stickers, and silly fun with your child like a potty dance!

You can also encourage your children to go by presenting them with big-kid underwear. Children are often in a hurry to grow up and be just like you, or the other kids they've seen and look up to. Having some on hand with cool designs may entice your child to engage with the training.

A tip for you, dads, give your child snacks that encourage urination — like salty snacks, food with high water content, and lots of water. The more often your child gets to practice with the potty, the faster the learning is going to take.

At night, don't be surprised if your child is still having some accidents. They're going to happen even with potty training. You'll want to use some waterproof sheets to be able to catch the urine before it reaches your child's mattress. Additionally, it's important you don't discipline your child for wetness. Complete potty training can take months, especially including nighttime dryness. Remember, your tot is impressionable and the muscles in their urinary floor aren't completely developed yet.

Tips For Training Boys

Firstly, you'll want to have potties with removable urine guards. It's true that these help protect your bathroom from a stray drizzle, but they can also scrape a boy's genitals when he sits down. This could make him hesitant to use the potty in the future.

Potty training your boy will require a degree of cooperation from him, and a lot of patience from you. Boys need to be interested in the act of potty training in order for it to be done effectively. Of course, they also need to be physically able. Boys can be ready for potty training as young as eighteen months old, however, this is the earliest estimate. It's not uncommon for boys to go untrained well past their third birthday. If your boy isn't ready yet, don't be too concerned.

Much of parents' statements that boys are difficult to potty-train are derived simply from the fact that they tried too early. Your boy will get it in his own time. Don't sweat it.

Start with sitting, and eventually move to standing for urine. In toddlers, bowel movements and urine come hand in hand. It'll take your child some time to develop the muscles needed to control both peeing and pooping separately. This will also discourage your son from getting cavalier with his spray! This will also help you with teaching him how to aim in the future.

When it comes to standing, your son can also learn by watching. Dads, don't be afraid to demonstrate to your child how to pee standing up. Your son will eventually want to try this for himself as his legs develop. When this time comes, make use of a permanent marker and draw a bulls' eye on the potty where he's supposed to be aiming. If you make a game of it, your boy will be much more interested. Trust me.

You may also need a stool at this point. Your boy may be tall enough to pee into the toilet or he may struggle. Gauge his needs based on his abilities. Just make sure the stool is sturdy and won't slip out from under him! You could install a hand guard for safety as well.

Tips For Training Girls

There's less to keep in mind with girls, but the process is nonetheless the same and will take as much time to perfect. Additionally, you won't have to remove any pee guards from their potties.

Girls tend to be more fond of a wider range of clothing than boys. From dresses, to skirts, to pants, and so on. You'll need to make sure your child knows how to hike her dresses up while she goes to prevent any errant wetness.

The most important thing with girls is to teach good wiping hygiene and etiquette. As girls' genitals are located quite close to their anus, teaching them to wipe from front to back will ensure that feces do not touch your child's bits. This will help prevent infections or any other health disasters that can arise from improper wiping for her.

When you move towards the toilet, you'll want to face girls forward on the toilet while placing a small stool under her feet to help her keep balance and prevent any slipping.

2

AGE 1

This chapter focuses entirely on the tot that's one-year-old, or close to this age developmentally. We'll also go over house childproofing to keep your little explorer safe as they satisfy their curiosities and learn about their environment. But first, things to understand and look out for.

Your child's physical growth and motor skills may start to slow in development at this point. Your child's energy is being committed internally now, to the development of their brains instead. Toddlerhood, or early childhood, involves tremendous leaps of growth in intellect, social skills, and emotional changes.

If by this point your child hasn't learned how to do certain things, like crawling, supported standing, speaking with simple words like "dada," isn't learning gestures, not pointing to things, or is even losing skills they had developed, you should take your child to your pediatrician for advice. There are many reasons for developmental delays in children, and it's better to be safe than sorry to weed out whether medical reasons may be one of them.

Pediatricians recommend you get your child tested for general development at nine, eighteen, and thirty months of age. They also say that you should have your child tested for autism at eighteen months of age and twenty for months of age, or if you're ever concerned that it is a factor. Pay attention to the way your child reacts to you and their environment — unresponsive children, or slow to respond children, may be influenced by unseen factors.

DEVELOPMENTAL MILESTONES AT AGE 1

You should be excited! Toddlerhood comes with a bunch of fun milestones and adorable moments. As your infant becomes a child, they will be capable of bonding with you on new levels.

Your toddler will begin to test the limits of the world around them — including you and perhaps your household pet. They want to see what they can get away with — something that can be equal parts adorable and frustrating. You should also expect a lot of hands-on learning.

Your toddler might be more grabby now. They'll be quite interested in long hair, in strings, and anything that dangles off you, really. You should expect, and prepare for, your child to be picking up many items and taste-testing them from time to time. Your toddler's pincer grips are how they start to develop their fine motor skills — those delicate, small movements requiring your fingers.

Until this point, your conversations with your child have been largely one-sided. From here, your kid will finally start to communicate with you in ways that you can understand. They'll use their words, showing off both their social and cognitive development. It'll take some time before the two of you are bantering together, but that time will come!

During this period of time, toddlers develop their vocabularies very quickly. That's because their brains are exceptionally pliable to new languages and skills during this period of time. If your family is bilingual, this is when you're going to want to start teaching your child both languages — it becomes much more difficult for your child to learn another language beyond the toddler stage. Toddlers will pick up new words by imitating the way their parents speak, so be aware of this as your toddler grows. If you want your tot not to swear, especially in multiple languages, don't swear in front of them!

Imitation comes into play with many of the activities that come with their care. You may notice your child attempting to brush their own hair, or their teeth. Take advantage of this developmental technique by establishing good habits for yourself and your child — like cleaning the house and practicing good hygiene.

Your child will certainly become a director at this stage as well. During play with you, they will tell you what role they want you to fill. Or, heartbreakingly, if they don't want to play with you.

Chances are, your kid will also begin to understand the concept of accomplishment. They'll know when they've done something special — even if it just happens to be in play. They'll look to you for applause, and may pause until they receive it from you.

Your toddler is beginning to understand that there is a sequence to how things work, but not necessarily that there are consequences for certain behaviors or series of events. Your child is still developing forethought — they may not yet understand that if you push a vase off a table, it will break, and they may get in trouble for it. Watch out to not let your child play with things that could harm them — such as doors. They may understand that a door swings open and shut, but not necessarily that they can hurt their hands by doing so recklessly.

Your kid will not associate pain with the actions they have taken. In fact, pain will come as a complete surprise to your kid. They will look to you for cues on how to react to certain situations, and if they see you worry, they may start crying. Your kid will need you to be vigilant for them at this stage until they begin to understand the concept of consequence, when they will be able to learn and remember those vital lessons.

With that said, do not overprotect your child. You should expect that small accidents will happen from time to time, and allow your child some room to explore safely. Your tot will need a lot of time to play outdoors. They'll also need a variety of ride-on toys, like beginner tricycles or cars they can push around with their feet. You should also keep some balls around, and some cardboard boxes on hand. Never underestimate the imaginative power of a toddler armed with a cardboard box.

Your tot will begin to develop hobbies as well. You may notice that your child will prefer one method of play over another. Perhaps you have a little athlete on your hands, or a little artist. Cultivate those by allowing them to spend more playtime doing those things, as long as they get a good amount of time doing other things as well.

Your toddler will be awake longer at this stage. You should be able to get two naps a day out of your one-year-old, or you may get none. Their sleepiness will diminish over the next few months as they grow used to your schedule and develop a circadian rhythm that helps them sleep through the night on a relatively consistent basis, if you're lucky.

If you're starting daycare, your daycare may operate on different napping schedules than you might've been planning for. Many daycares offer only one nap time a day. This is okay, and it's not something to worry about. You'll both get used to the new schedule, or you can shift when your tot takes a second nap — as long as you don't nap too close to bedtime.

Don't forget to celebrate the first birthday! Dads, it's likely your child will not remember this birthday. This day is probably more exciting for you than what it is for your baby. Use it as a day to have a little party with your child, and celebrate all your hard work during the first year of being a dad! You've earned it.

To Daycare or Not to Daycare

After the first year of life, daycare becomes available. Daycare is a great way to introduce your one-year-old to new environments and social settings, which will aide them in developing their socialization skills like empathy and teamwork. This will also be a great way for your tot to make friends, and for you to make bonds with other parents for playdates in the future.

With that being said, there are also benefits to stay-at-home care. Your child may not be ready to face the challenges being around a large crowd of other children poses to them, so they may need to be kept back from daycare until they develop more confidence with crowds. There is some evidence to suggest that more parental interaction with children throughout this stage is also beneficial to the child. It's recommended that stay-at-home parents try to get their child active with at least one-on-one interaction with a child their age, as early socialization is crucial.

If you choose to daycare, this likely means you can return to work. Fathers are often working throughout infancy, but if you're the primary caregiver, it's likely you've been off work for a year while your child progresses through the delicate baby stages.

Many parents will choose whether or not daycare or stay-at-home parenting is the right fit for them based on financial ability. This is fair — you're going to need plenty of funds for the coming years, and money does not grow on trees. Or maybe you just crave the routine of work again, as many parents do. Discuss with your partner about which options will work best for you and your family.

The Signs of an Overtired Tot

While your tot will certainly be sleeping less in general, sometimes this sleeplessness is derived from factors not necessarily related to not being tired. In fact, sometimes your tot isn't sleeping because they're overtired.

Over-tiredness is not a problem for toddlers alone. Chances are, you've experienced this a few times over the first year of your baby's life! We've certainly all had nights where it was hard to stay asleep for the full recommended seven to eight hours. You may notice that even after pulling an all-nighter, you feel fully awake. You are, in fact, not.

Your toddler is the same. Overtired tots will have a harder time falling and staying asleep. You may also notice that your child's eyelids will twitch if they've been awake too long, or they're rubbing their eyes. They could also be pulling on their ears of hair. Their balance and wobbliness may be exaggerated, and they're likely yawning every few minutes.

Overtired toddlers tend to be cranky toddlers, too. Most people tend to be cranky when they're sleepless, but with your toddler this may look like screaming, crying, or hitting. As your baby has grown, you will have noticed they have different cries to signal their different needs. They have a tired cry as well. This cry tends to be preceded by an "owh" noise that sounds much like a yawn, followed by a soft cry that gradually ascends in volume. This cry can sound similar to the hungry cry as well. You'll be able to tell the difference based on the preceding sounds your baby makes, as well as whether or not your child has eaten recently. For safety, you can give your baby a snack and then take a nap — sometimes the snacking helps your child fall asleep as well.

To keep your child asleep, you need to follow a consistent schedule and expend your baby's energy. Exercise is a great way to tire your tot out, and will help them stay asleep.

If exercise isn't enough to keep your tot asleep, you can try other calming strategies. Maybe your child needs some company while they try to fall asleep. Cuddle with your child, maybe even read to them softly to encourage sleepiness. Your child may simply be staying awake because they want to be with you. If this is the case, maybe you could even take a nap with your child!

Having a consistent bedtime routine every night will also help trigger the baby's brain to produce the sleepy chemicals. The act of practicing self-hygiene every night, like brushing your teeth, your hair, or having a show encourages your body to relax after a long day. This is advice that you can use, too, if you have trouble with sleeping. Your toddler will likely be sleepless for many of the same reasons you are.

Another example of behaviors that can keep you and your baby awake is having screen time or overstimulation before sleep times. Television, phones and computers are all fun things to use, but the use of them will likely stave off feelings of tiredness. There are a few reasons for this. Blue light from the screens triggers your brain to feel awake and alert. There's also the simple fact that those things come with fun and interesting programs one could spend hours on — TV shows, games, what have you. You should try to limit your baby's exposure to these before bedtime, and move to quieter areas in the house where you can do activities like reading.

You may have used swaddling as a method to help your baby sleep. At one-years-old, this technique is still useful. Holding your toddler swaddle in a dark or dimly lit room with no sound or stimulation can help encourage sleep.

Stress can also keep your toddler awake. If you have an unstable household, or your child is not securely attached to you or your partner, this can manifest in a child's inability to feel safe and fall asleep.

CHILDPROOFING YOUR HOME

One of the biggest concerns you and your partners should have from day one of being parents is childproofing your home. By now, you've likely already gone through the childproofing process in your home that is well enough for infancy. However, as your toddler begins to explore and come into their own, your needs for childproofing will be much more extensive.

With the right childproofing gadgets, you can significantly reduce the odds of bumps and bruises. Your rooms are likely going to need to be reorganized — important tech and wires lifted out of reach of curious fingertips. A little forethought into how you keep your room and your furniture will go a long way to keep your baby safe!

You can start with cushioning the sharp edges of your furniture — like your tables or chairs — with bumpers, which can soften any accidental impacts. Every room in your house with hazardous materials, such as bathrooms and kitchens, should be blocked off with baby gates or plastic door knob covers.

Your best baby gate options are multi-use and extra tall. They should extend enough to secure to the walls well enough that even you can't shake them out. Having baby gates that are wide and adjustable will be your best bet.

To be extra safe, keep your cleaning supplies well out of reach of your child. You can move these up to high cupboards or put them in rooms your toddler will be blocked from entering — like a basement closet or in your garage. You'll want to keep your medications and alcohol in locked closets away from the floor as well.

You could also consider metal window guards. These screw into the sides of your window frame (some window frames have holes for you to do this), but be sure that they have bars no more than four inches apart.

THE CHILDPROOFING CHECKLIST

Below is a checklist that you can use to get started with childproofing your home. Your home may have needs that are not considered in this book, so be sure that you're careful to analyze your home for yourselves.

For the Home:

- Anchor your television to the wall, and hide electrical cords. You should also hide non-electrical cords, like HDMI cables or AUX cables.
- Move any technology from low shelves to high shelves. Better yet, anchor them to the wall if you can.
- Get window coverings and baby gate covers installed, so your child can't tamper with them.
- Install carbon monoxide and smoke detectors on every floor. In many places, houses are built to have these pre-installed. However, you may still want to check the batteries (if applicable) and update them regularly.
- Purchase fire extinguishers. Fire safety is tantamount to keeping your home safe for your child. Learn how to use the various different types of fire extinguishers and make sure you keep them in easily accessible locations in case of emergency.
- Don't have corded phones near where the baby can reach. Keep cordless phones if you can. Or do away with landlines, and just keep a cellphone.

- Stock your medicine cabinets and first-aid kits.
- Remove blinds with looped cords.
- Place baby gates at the top and bottom of stairs.
- Install childproofed door knobs that little hands can't squeeze to open.
- Install childproof locks.
- Limit the space your baby can explore to a room where you can easily monitor your child.
- Move tall and wobbly lamps behind furniture.
- Do away with any breakable objects, such as vases.
- Remove anything that can be knocked off of tables or bookshelves, for your child's and your property's safety.
- Install fireplace screens around your hearths.
- Put safety covers over electrical outlets.
- Keep your smaller gadgets well out of reach and your floors clean.
- Do away with flaking or peeling paint on your walls, especially if you have a particularly old house. Houses built before 1978 may still have lead paint, which you

should also remove as best as you can. Lead paint is harmful to ingest, and the dust particles of lead paint will have serious lasting cognitive effects on your child.

- Latch any ground-level doors, especially in your kitchen and bathroom areas where chemicals are kept. Any chemicals that are harmful should be stored in areas your baby can't feasibly access. These are things like detergents, bleach, and many other laundry essentials.
- Put non-slip pads under your rugs.
- Cover all sharp edges and corners on your furniture with bumpers or safety padding.
- Unplug small appliances when not in use. Make sure plugs are locked away or those appliances are moved into cupboards or drawers.
- Do away with table cloths.
- Get stove knob covers and cook on your back burners.
- Have lockable covers on your garbage cans, if you keep those in open spaces and not behind lockable doors.
- Have your crib away from all other furniture.

- Install safety guards on your windows.
- Remove your crib mobile.
- Secure dresses and bookshelves to the wall.

For the Car:

- Brush up on your car seat safety basics. Only use approved rear-facing car seats in the back seat. A local certified child passenger safety technician will approve your seat for free.
- Keep any electrical appliances or wires in your glove box.
- Keep tissues on hand.
- Keep any (small) garbage bags in the front of the vehicle. These will be nice to have with you, in case of any accidents. You can use plastic shopping bags for this.
- Keep a wealth of tools in your car in case of emergency. Some tools you should consider: a utility knife with a safety belt cutter, scissors, a phone charger, a map.
- Keep a first aid kit in the trunk of your vehicle or in your glove box/passenger seat away from your child.
- Enable your car's childproof door locks.

These make sure your doors only open from the outside.

- Engage your window locks.
- Secure unused seatbelts by removing them from the seats or tucking them between cushions and out of view.
- Apply stick-on sun shades to the back windows to block the rays of the sun. Avoid ones that connect with suction cups, or are loose, as those can easily fall or be pulled off. You really want to stick with the stick-on ones, as they are safer for your child and exploring hands won't be able to pry them off.
- Keep your car clean and tidy. Remove any small objects that could be choking hazards, like coins and pens.
- Get your vehicle safety checked and your seat belts checked.
- Get your child seats safety checked and that they are age-appropriate. You will need to replace your car crib and upgrade to a seat, which you'll need to replace as your child grows.
- Invest in a portable diaper pad.
- Have some back seat organizers on the floor

of your car where you can store toys, treats, extra clothes, blankets.

- Have a mirror installed on your car seat that you can view from your rearview mirror. Have this situated in such a way that you can see your child.
- Always check your car before you begin driving. Ensure your tires are well treaded, your breaks are in good working order, your oil is changed, your lights are working, your battery is charged, and all other belts, tubes, and fluid levels are good.
- Keep foldable back seats locked into their upright positions.

One other thing you could consider is installing a car seat monitor. These have the benefit of being able to keep a close eye on your child, and some of the more expensive ones can allow you to see that your car seat is secure throughout the trip. This isn't a necessity, however. You do still have your car mirror!

You should never leave your child unattended in your vehicle. This is unsafe for many reasons, especially during the summer. You should ensure that your patience extends to your driving and that you are not an angry driver. Additionally, you should follow your local traffic laws to the last detail. You should also avoid eating in the car, as this is a distraction.

Never drink and drive.

The BABIES Mindset Program for Babyproofing Your Home

A good acronym to keep in mind while you get your house into prime toddler shape is BABIES.

1. **Be** vigilant.
2. **A**void breakable objects.
3. **B**eware of poisons and other harmful substances.
4. **I**dentify and fix any issues in your home.
5. **E**xamine all spaces the baby comes in contact with.
6. **S**tay nearby, so you can intervene before an accident happens.

If you keep this mindset, nothing will escape your fatherly focus.

DAD ANXIETY

Now that we've gone through all the things that could possibly go wrong and the ways that the world can end, you might be feeling like there's a thousand things you're going to need to watch out for. You must be very anxious. This is healthy to a certain degree — it shows you're taking this seriously — but you also need to make sure that you're taking a step back to calm down.

Anxious minds struggle to fix and analyze problems. It's very common for dads, any parents really, to feel overwhelmed by all the things they're just now realizing could endanger their children. When you're used to living in certain ways, you take advantage of the fact that you know better to get hurt. But babies? That's a whole other level of consideration you're going to have to keep in mind.

Keeping a list of all the things you've got to do will help put your childproofing duties into perspective, and this is a technique used often to help people cope with their anxieties in general. Lists are extremely helpful for remembering your jobs for you as well.

Keep in mind that you're only human. You're not a bad father for not having everything squared away from day one. In fact, you're a good father for thinking about how to fix up your place to keep your child safe.

If you're lucky enough to be reading this before your child is one, then you have some time to prepare. Start today, so that you can get all the basic and fundamental requirements of babyproofing sealed away.

The good news is that you'll only have to live in a childproof house for a temporary amount of time. You'll be able to ease up on certain safety precautions as your child grows to understand their environment and the concept of consequences. Of course, with age comes other concerns, but you've got this, Dads.

3

AGE 2

ou may have heard the term "the terrible twos." This is the span of time ranging between two and three years of age, defined by a child's growing tendency to push boundaries with you and others. We'll discuss this more at length at the end of the next chapter, but what you need to understand for now is that the struggles from these years are a good thing.

As a father, you should want your child to explore and push their limits. That's the only way they can learn after all! While it may make your life difficult at times, any moment that can be turned into a teachable one is a great thing.

During this chapter, we will discuss the changes that come as your one-year-old turns two. We'll go over the developmental milestones you can expect from a two-year-old, the first stages of independence, and games you can play with your child to help develop their fine motor skills. We'll also cover the responsibilities your child may be capable of handling at this age!

DEVELOPMENTAL MILESTONES AT AGE 2

Keep in mind while reading through these developmental milestones that every child is different. It is important to speak with your pediatrician if your two-year-old hasn't reached one-year-old milestones, but don't be too concerned if your child hasn't reached the two-year-old milestones yet. More specifically, if your child doesn't use two-word phrases, doesn't know what to do with common items like spoons, doesn't try to copy your actions or words, follow instructions, can't walk steadily, or if their skills regress, you will want to speak to your child's doctor.

At two years of age, your child will be going through a ton of social, emotional, cognitive, language, and physical development.

You may notice your monkey doing everything you do or doing everything older children do. Your child has learned now that mimicking others is the best way for them to develop their skills, so they will do it often! They are more impressionable now, so be sure not to use any questionable gestures. The last thing you need is a two-year-old that knows how to flip the bird.

Your two-year-old will demonstrate more excitement when around other children. By now, your child's shyness should have receded enough that they can interact and make friends with their peers. Your child will mostly play alongside those friends at this stage, which you should be used to. However, you may begin to notice your child participating in simple games with other kids — like chase games.

Your kid's brain is as absorbent as ever, especially with language and communication. Your child is picking up on body language cues. They will be able to point to things or pictures where they are named, and may be able to name them themselves! On average, you can expect kids at this age to say short two to four-word sentences. Your child should also be able to follow simple instructions like, "Go get it!"

or "Come here!" In conversation, your toddler will repeat words they've overheard, even just in passing.

On the cognitive side of things, your two-year-old is developing the ability to find things that have been hidden away. Even if those objects are covered by a few things! Your child will begin to distinguish between shapes and colors, and will be able to sort them. In familiar books, your child will be able to complete the sentences or rhymes.

If your child is the building type, you'll notice them starting to erect towers all over your house with four or more blocks! Luckily, your child will be able to understand you when you give them instructions to pick up their toys and put them in their bin. You'll also notice your children are engaging in much more pretend play.

You'll also notice the development of handedness. Your child will begin to prefer one hand over the other.

There are a lot of small and huge physical milestones your two-year-old will be reaching soon. Your kid should be able to stand on their tiptoes soon, jump, kick a ball, start running. It's possible they may even learn to balance solely on one foot. They're going to be able to climb onto furniture and get off of it without help! They'll be able to ascend stairs and throw balls overhanded.

The First Stages of Independence

The early years of childhood should be joyful for your whole family. Being two comes with leaps and bounds of growth — your child will walk, talk, laugh, sing, and gain new life experiences every day. Your child will have favorite foods and activities. They'll have things they like and dislike. Opinions!

You should be proud to see your child coming into their own like this. While these remarkable advances in their sense of self are truly beautiful, they come with an increased struggle for independence between the ages of two and three. What you should understand for now is that you should foster your child's desire to be independent by empowering them to take part in the act of caring for themselves.

You should be giving your child opportunities to be independent by allowing them to carry their things. Your child is fully capable of carrying their lunch boxes, and putting their toys away. They can clean up after themselves, and put things where they belong. You should invite your child to help with chores by putting their laundry into drawers and doing other simple tasks.

During these early years, you should allow your child to participate in the following for sure:

1. Tooth brushing. Good oral hygiene habits are crucial to develop at this stage.
2. Dressing and undressing. Clothes are one of the number one ways people express themselves, so allow your child to participate in this action!
3. Handwashing. This is another crucial hygiene and life skill, especially in today's environment. Effective handwashing saves lives.
4. Household chores, such as:
5. Picking up toys and putting them away.
6. Sweeping with a small broom and a dustpan.
7. Dusting with a feather duster or a cloth. Never use chemical cleaners and make sure breakable objects are out of reach. You should supervise this as your child wipes tables with a rag and a spritz bottle.
8. Setting and clearing the table. For this, you want to make sure your dishware is

unbreakable. Don't let your child pick up the knives.

9. Water plants in the home and garden.
10. Fetch or deliver mail. Or bringing other lightweight and safe items around the home.
11. Help in the kitchen by mixing batter, tearing lettuce, washing produce, putting salads together, and using certain cookie cutters.

Getting your child into the habit of doing these things will help them develop healthier habits later on in life. Children who play active roles in caring for their home and their hygiene grow into adults with keen senses of cleanliness. This has a number of obviously good connotations, but lesser known, it also improves the chances of good mental health in the future.

Kicking the Thumb-Sucking Habit

Many children grow up with sucking habits. Whether their object of focus is their thumb or a pacifier, you can expect that your child's going to want to have something in their mouths. Thumb-sucking is a self-soothing action children use to comfort themselves when they feel hungry, afraid, quiet, sleepy, bored, or otherwise restless.

Thumb-sucking in children under four is not seen as much of an issue. After this time, however, vigorous suckers can put themselves at risk of dental or speech issues. With this in mind, it's important to urge your child to stop sucking on their thumbs or pacifiers when you can feasibly do so. While there's usually no urgency, this will save you a lot of concern in the future.

The best way to wean your child off this habit is to set rules and provide distractions to your child. You can limit the times and places your child is allowed to suck their thumbs. You may find some benefit in putting away items that play into your child's thumb-sucking behavior, like toys they sleep with or blankets. You can also make use of gloves as a more direct barrier to stop thumb-sucking.

To kick the habit, your child will need a lot of praise and positive attention. You should reward your child for not thumb-sucking as much as you can. Something you could do to reward your child would be to give them stickers on a calendar for every day they didn't suck their thumbs. Maybe even have a little party for your child after a certain number of days!

Remember that this behavior isn't perceived as an issue in children who are preschool age or younger. Your child's doctors may not even bother with the behavior until after this point. As it's seldom an issue, don't worry too much if your treatments aren't immediately effective. Many tots grow out of this behavior on their own eventually.

THE MINE PHASE

As a father, you've already gotten used to sharing much of your space and things with your child. You're glad to do so! But, you've started to notice something in your child. Things that don't belong to them, even things they might not even know what they are for, suddenly fall under the tot's canopy of "mine." Doesn't matter what it is.

"My" and "mine" are some of the first words your child will use to describe the world around them. In the eyes of a toddler, the first person to find and stake claim to something is the rightful owner of that thing. Your toddler will believe that anyone who finds an object first is its rightful owner, a stage that will last from shortly before your tot hits two to around four years of age.

While this is, admittedly, one of the least charming phases of your tot, it's a good thing. Your toddler is beginning to understand that there are invisible ties between people and a thing. This points to a slowly sophisticating sense of self in your child. You can't have a sense of "mine" without first having a sense of "me."

Evidence suggests that toddlers go through this stage as part of the process of figuring out who they are. It follows, too, that the stuff we own as adults is also linked to ourselves. This is a behavioral term called the "endowment effect," which suggests that objects we own are more valuable to us simply because we own them. We have an emotional attachment to things that are ours. Your toddler is in the beginning stages of developing this.

While your toddler will get confused from time to time about what is theirs, if you tell them what is theirs explicitly, then they will remember that in the future. Children will be able to distinguish which toys are theirs, even if they look similar to other toys and objects that belong to someone else. Even if the toys are the exact same, your toddler will say that they enjoy their toy better as well.

To help your child learn, you should explain the rules to them. Your toddler isn't misbehaving purposefully by staking a claim — they're trying to figure out right and wrong, and what the rules of their environment are. Additionally, you don't always have to teach your child to share.

If there are particularly precious toys that your child enjoys and doesn't want to share with others, you should expect your child to stand up for themselves if another child tries to snatch them away. You wouldn't want someone picking up your phone, right? Just be sure to watch out for this, as your child may be inclined to voice their frustrations more loudly than you would like.

THE IMPORTANCE OF PLAY

Among many animals, play is absolutely crucial. For primates, play is so embedded in our biological roots that it is our main method of learning as infants and toddlers. Humans and other apes are not the only animals to use play, either. Dogs, cats, and all sorts of animals — even birds — use play to understand the world around them.

Play at all stages of development is important for the growth of your child's imagination, dexterity, and their physical, cognitive, and emotional strength. It is an exceedingly healthy aspect of brain development. Play will factor into your child's lives for the rest of their lives! It's also important for social, physical, and cognitive development.

Play is the first way your child learns to interact with the world. For your tot, play is their best friend to mastering their world. Play allows your child to develop new competencies, which then leads to confidence and self-resilience to face future challenges. Keeping your child from play has serious developmental consequences, so it's important to allow your child to play as much as they can.

It's ideal that most of playtime involves adult and parental participation. Play is the ideal opportunity for you to engage with your child! On top of being able to teach your child with play, it's good for your health as well. Fun fact, playing with your child releases oxytocin in the brain — the hormone which plays a huge role in parent-infant bonding, also known as the "love" chemical. For both you and your child, you should strive to find a healthy play-work balance that suits your child's' social and academic needs.

In today's hurried life, it's important to set aside an abundance of time for your child to play. It's no secret that there's less and less time nowadays for parents to be able to spend with their child, with increasing demands for work and career life demanding parents to spend less time with their families and more time at the desk. This is an unfortunate reality of many of our lives. You'll have to do your best to find a schedule for play that works for you and your child, and consider a babysitter even if you're working from home!

Remember, you'll never look back on these years and think, "I spent too much time playing with my child." Don't be afraid to set as much time as you can aside for your tot! There's no such thing as too much play.

Undirected Play

Though you may want to structure and schedule out every second to guide the flow of your child's play, it's important that you allow your tot the freedom to play on their own terms. Undirected play leads to better teamwork abilities, as well as sharing, negotiating, conflict resolution and self-advocating skills.

Your child will practice their decision-making skills, move at their own pace, and discover new areas of interest. It's through undirected play that your child learns more about themselves — you'll even notice the emergence of new hobbies and passions.

When adults rules are incorporated into the playtime, your child will be missing out on many of the benefits of play — the development of creativity, leadership and group skills, to name a few.

You should encourage unstructured play as much as possible. There's nothing wrong with the occasional game with rules, but your main form of play with your child should be unstructured. Unstructured play is also an exceptional way to increase your child's physical activity in general! Children tend to want to get all their energy out by moving their bodies around, so if you let them be, the chances are they'll be running around your yard to burn some off!

Play Ball

Balls are a very versatile and useful toy. They can be used in many different ways that can help your little one develop a slew of skills and learn new concepts. At this age, ball play helps children develop their grasping skills, their hand-eye coordination, visual tracking, and strength in their finger muscles. Your child will also develop better cognitive understanding of the ball and its materials; they will develop the understanding that the balls bounce, roll, are easy to move but sometimes difficult to keep still.

Throwing and catching are two skills that begin development in the toddlerhood stage. You'll notice that your tot is attempting their first throw anywhere between 12 and 18 months of age! This will slowly progress to holding the ball from the chest and throwing it that way, to gentle underhanded tosses later on in childhood. Your child will learn to catch the ball by hugging it to their chest first. With some practice, this will develop into catching with only their hands later.

Catching practice is one of the hallmark activities you can make use of while supporting your toddler's gross motor skill development. Playing a gentle game of catch with a larger ball made of soft materials is a great way to begin this. You could even start by simply rolling the ball towards your tot, depending on their development until this point. A fun challenge you can pose to your child is to try to get them to roll or toss the ball into a cardboard box, moving it farther and farther away as your child masters the activity.

If it takes your child some time to master the ball, that's totally okay. Even some adults aren't necessarily the best throwers or the best catchers. Your toddler will eventually come to understand the basic principles of throwing and catching in ball play. Every child develops at her own pace, and if your toddler isn't throwing fastballs by 18 months, it's not a cause for concern.

4

AGE 3

"*L*et me do it!"

You're probably incredibly acquainted with this saying by now. Your two-year-old was absolutely convinced that they were a big eight-year-old and that they could tackle the world on their own, and your three-year-old will be no different.

Most parents tend to say that the three-year-old mark is the time when parenting challenges start to ramp up in difficulty. This is due to your child's growing independence and desire to test the rules, and you. Never fear, though. You've gotten this far, dads!

This chapter goes over all the developmental milestones you can expect from your three-year-old. It will also teach you more about the observation side of proper guidance as your child shows clear signs of physical changes, and habit building.

DEVELOPMENTAL MILESTONES AT AGE 3

Your three-year-old is continuing to develop their brain more than they are their bodies. While your child should be able to climb well, run easily, and walk up and down stairs all on their own, the development they're experiencing is still internal! That being said, one fun part of raising your three-year-old is that they can finally pedal a real tricycle on their own, as opposed to those push tricycles you may have used when your child was one.

Children are starting to look more distinct now than other children. After age 2, children of the same age can noticeably vary in height and weight. Your child won't notice this as much as you do, but you'll start to be able to notice more who your child takes after!

Your child likely has all 20 primary, or "baby," teeth. Their vision is nearing 20/20. It is around this point that you will be able to notice any discrepancies in their teeth or vision, such as if teeth are coming in crooked or if vision is not growing as well as you expect it to. Your pediatrician will want to keep an eye on these, and you should as well.

Your child's emotional expression is deepening. You will notice more sophisticated reactions and interactions from your three-year-old. Without prompting, your three-year-old will begin to show their affection for you and for their friends. This will look like hugging or kissing, or even showing concern for the people around them if they're upset. If your child's friend is crying, you'll notice that your child is there for them!

Your child's emotional expression will also develop well in this stage. Subtle body language cues will begin to tip your child off to how you're feeling, and your child will also begin to utilize them.

By now, it's likely you've developed a schedule with your child that both of you have gotten used to. Now, your child will expect to stay on this schedule. Any deviations from their schedule may result in some upsetness, especially if those changes are major. This includes any changes to new additions to routine — like your tot dressing themselves. They may want the independence of doing their routine themselves.

This is because your toddler is beginning to develop a sense of self. Your tot understands that their name, age, and gender link into who they are as people — and they'll begin to identify themselves this way. They'll also be able to distinguish who others are by naming their friends. You'll hear a lot more "I"s and "me"s out of your child as well. They'll also be able to carry on simple conversations using two or three sentences, and will talk fairly well with strangers.

Following more complex instructions (with two or three steps) becomes much easier for your child. They'll also be able to name familiar things, and understand words like "in", "on," and "under." Their understanding of concepts like "lateness," and "more," will also develop. Your child will be able to understand around 500 to 900 words — more if you practiced reading with them often. They'll begin to use words like "please," and "thank you" much more often.

Interesting developments in problem-solving, creativity, and the use of tools will arise here as well. Your tot will begin to work with buttons, levers, and moving parts. They'll play much more. Your child will play a bunch of make believe with dolls, animals, and people. Numerical recognition will start to come into play as well — your child will be able to understand basic numbers, like one and two. All in all, your child will be able to concentrate on tasks for around eight to nine minutes, though multitasking is not their strong suit!

Where it comes to speech specifically, this may take some time to come to fruition. While your child may know plenty of things, speech develops at a rate of its own. This is an incredibly exciting bit to parenting a three-year-old, as you'll be able to witness your child's garbled words transform and become clear. Depending on your child, this can start happening slower or faster. Ensure that you're speaking often with your child, and enunciating their messy words back to them. At this point, you may notice the beginnings of an accent.

On average, children will have control of their bladders and bowels by this time. They can use the potty chair or toilet, depending on their size. You may want to keep your child's potty around if they are on the smaller side, to prevent any unwanted toilet diving.

Three-year-olds will generally have an established circadian rhythm. They will sleep anywhere between 11 and 13 hours a night, and you should not be alarmed if they sleep even a touch longer or need a nap through the day.

Challenges to Pose to Your Three-Year-Old

Now that your tike is three, you can start to have them interact more in the process of developing themselves. You should encourage your child to engage with you while you show them how things work, like asking you questions. Whenever you notice your child is interested in something, talk to them about it and teach them about it. If you notice your child isn't interested in something, try to generate interest with your own excitement.

You've been the one telling the stories up until now, but it's time for a change. You should ask your children to weave tales for you, or to start trying to read out books for themselves to you.

Encouraging your child at this stage to participate in the act of reading, writing and drawing is crucial to developing your child's creativity. Additionally, with writing and drawing, you can support your child's hand-eye coordination for the future. Music and dance is another great way to do this! Get your child as involved with these activities as they like.

Getting your child involved in the arts is a great way to teach your child expression and how to handle their feelings. The arts have innately cathartic effects on the brain when they are done in unstructured ways. You can also use the arts with your child to demonstrate different expressions — what happiness looks like, what sadness looks like, surprise, and so on.

Some form of the arts, like music and writing, also teach your children more words. If you're raising a bilingual child, having them listen to songs in both languages and read books in both languages is a great way to support their language development.

You'll begin to notice that your child can accomplish much more with their hands. To help develop this, have your child unscrew and screw jar lids, or turn door handles. In fact, you should let your child do as much for themselves as they want to handle. Supervise your child brushing their teeth, washing their hands, and combing their hair — to make sure they're doing it properly. Otherwise, allow them to be independent with as much as they want to try for themselves, as long as these activities are safe.

Since your child has basic numerical recognition, challenge them by counting to ten with them. Start slow to build up their skills! You may also want to use some form of object to distinguish between the numbers. Blocks work well for this activity!

POSITIVE PARENTING

Most parents often become confused and frustrated by the challenges of parenthood. Aside from those that happen at home, there's a lot of confusion regarding the best ways to raise a child. What was common practice even twenty years ago, like spanking, has fallen well out of favor today and has been proven to have incredibly damaging effects on the child.

That's why it's difficult to know the right ways to raise your child. You might be inclined to follow in your own parents' footsteps, even if it includes practices that have been largely discredited today through research. You turned out fine, you might think. And while that can certainly be true, your child is not you.

One of the important components of being prepared as a parent is to understand childhood development.

No one's asking you to have a degree in early learning, but it does help to understand the milestones of development and the physical and socio-emotional challenges your child will be facing. Knowing these will arm you with realistic expectations for each stage, and you'll be able to pre-emptively plan how to deal with the challenges that define those stages.

All stages of development come with their own unique challenges, and this persists all the way through to adulthood. The idea that each stage has a key psychosocial challenge to overcome is one that's existed since psychology was founded as a field. You may have heard of Erikson's theories regarding the stages of psychosocial development, which included emotional challenges at key stages in your child's life. While the truth of development is not quite so clear-cut as Erikson and other psychoanalysts believed hundreds of years ago, there is some universality to development. While the timing may be different for each child, your child will pick up on language eventually.

One of the most popular theories of parenting psychology stems from positive psychology, a theory which existed for a hundred years but was named first by Maslow in his book *Motivation and Personality*. The key difference to positive psychology to other theories is its focus on what works rather than on what's broken.

Enter Positive Parenting

Positive parenting comes from positive psychology, which is considered the best method of raising your children in the family psychology field. Positive psychology focuses on happiness, resilience, and youth development. Parenting research has moved away from deficits and risk factors to focusing on predictors of positive outcomes, for example, protective factors. This style of parenting exemplifies the approach of seeking to promote parenting behaviors that are essential for youth development, such as caring, teaching, leading, communicating, reasoning, and providing.

Emotional warmth, consistency, sensitivity, and boundary setting are the capstone tenets of this style of parenting. Your child is a growing person and should be respected as an individual as you'd respect any adult. That means giving your child space to make mistakes, learn from mistakes, and adhere to the rules. It also means giving your child emotional space when they need it, their privacy, and so on.

Proactively teaching your child should be coupled with inductive discipline and parental involvement in your child's activities. The support that comes from a present and engaged parent that's sensitive to their child comes paired with better cognitive functioning, which translates to better school adjustment, fewer behavior issues, and better self-image.

Gottman's Five Steps

John M. Gottman, Ph.D., focused much of his research in childhood development around the tenets of positive psychology. His writings are highly influential now in the discussions about childhood development. He developed a five-step "emotional coaching" method which teaches new parents the things they need to be mindful of while raising their tot. These are as follows:

1. awareness of emotions
2. connecting with your child
3. listening to your child
4. naming emotions
5. finding solutions (Gottman, 1997)

Live by those guidelines when it comes to parenting your child. You need to understand that you're not just raising anything, you're raising another human being. Before you know it, they're going to have a life outside of you. They're going to have personalities that weren't wholly from you, too.

That's a good thing, and you should support this development as much as possible by embracing Gottman's Five Steps.

When you use the Five Steps, you will learn how to be more empathically aware of your child and their needs. It'll help you keep a calm demeanor when something goes wrong as well.

The "Terrible" Years

Beginning from age two and extending through to age three are the years dubbed the "Terrible Twos." Your child doesn't have the years of experience dealing with their emotions that you do, and heightened emotions and over stimulation tend to result in one thing for tots: temper tantrums.

When your child is in the midst of a total nuclear meltdown, it's important to take a step back. You want to yell less and to love more. Yelling is a defense mechanism, but it's not a productive one in this case (or in any case), and should never be used. Especially with your child. Even if they're yelling.

Labeling your child's behavior helps them understand what they're doing that's not okay, even if it seems like you're not getting through to them. Don't get angry or impatient, but do be honest with your child about what their behavior is doing and how it's not okay.

Making your expectations for behavior explicitly clear is important. You should create a list of family rules that everyone in your home has discussed and agreed to. When your child disobeys, you can step in to teach obedience — children are not naturally born obedient, they need to be taught to respect the rules. This can be easier said than done, however. It requires a lot of persistence and patience. You can expect that your child will break rules and perhaps often. Like adults, children have patterns of misbehavior.

Understanding those patterns will help you nip them in the bud before another meltdown can happen. Being emotionally attuned to your little one is crucial to raising an emotionally healthy child. If you're able to recognize your child's needs at any given moment, this will help you navigate around a meltdown situation before it can even happen.

When your child does end up misbehaving in destructive physical ways, like throwing food or banging on your keyboard or knocking things over, then you'll need to address this behavior directly. You should give your child your full attention in frequent, small doses, so that your child doesn't act out like this for your attention. If that fails, then it's time to redirect your tot.

Lovingly shift your child to a different activity. Maybe it's as easy as giving them a toy to play with or putting something on the television for them to watch while you finish what you're doing. Many children act out because they're not being stimulated — they're bored. Give them something to do and you'll find many of the tantrums tend to resolve themselves.

When you're dealing with the fallout of a meltdown, it's important to embrace patience and the love you have for your child. You want to praise your child more often than you correct — even as much as ten times more often, but in the right ways. Remember those stickers?

Create a behavior sticker chart. Listen, stickers will never be as powerful again as they are when your child is 3. You want to take advantage of that fact as much as you can during these years. You'll want to be praising effort as well. In fact, praise effort more than you praise outcome. This is important, as children may go feeling like their efforts aren't worth it if they're consistently criticized throughout them. You may have even felt this once or twice as an adult, so be sure to be sensitive to this.

Make sure that you're meeting the emotional needs of your child with touch. Three-year-olds need lots of hugs and snuggles. Touch is extremely important and healthy, and contributes to stability in mental health and self-image when it is provided. This is true at all stages of life, but especially for children.

Be consistent. With both of these methods of caring for a toddler's meltdown combined, applied on a regular basis, you will be cutting much of the difficulty out for you and your child. You never want to regress to yelling or harsh punishments, but stick to the expectations listed here patiently. You need to make sure that whenever the problem behavior returns that you rise to challenge it. Don't let one instance go without your attention. This will teach your child that pushing and misbehavior won't get them their way.

When all else fails, then you can resort to a timeout. Remember, timeouts are a good way to teach your child how to de-escalate for themselves. It'll be harder to convince your child to go to timeout at this stage. If you ask your child, and they're defiant, then you'll probably have to pick them up and set them in the timeout zone yourself. As soon as their temper tantrum has finished, then end the timeout. Don't let your child stay in timeout longer than it takes for them to calm down.

It's worth mentioning that you're probably not the only person providing childcare at this stage. In fact, you might have a few people looking after your child depending on the day. If you have a partner, or a parent who splits custody, you'll want to communicate your plans for action with them. You'll also want to discuss how you've been treating your child's behavior with your babysitters and early childhood educators, the latter of which you may or may not have, depending on your area's laws regarding starting kindergarten.

All of your caregivers should know what you're doing to reward your child's behavior, especially.

Make sure that they have access to your stickers and charts, and any other reward you may be using!

Lastly, don't expect to go through these years all on your own. You want to be your child's Superman and no one can blame you for that. But even Superman needs a break once in a while. Make sure that you're taking care of your own emotional needs and that you're asking for help when you need to. Every Superman has his Justice League. There's no shame in asking for backup!

5

AGE 4

What the heck just happened? You remember setting your kid down to sleep last night and when you went to wake them up this morning they'd grown four inches overnight. You weren't prepared to overhaul the wardrobe again — and just how much is your child planning on growing by tomorrow?

At first glance, the development of your four-year-old tot is defined by a period of increased growth and coordination. Your child will begin to express themselves in longer and more complicated sentences! And they're going to tell you what's what with those sentences. They may start tattling as well.

This chapter focuses on the development of your four-year-old. At this age, your child is beginning to have rudimentary understandings of reason and communication will flow much better between the two of you. Your child will be capable of having more responsibilities as they come upon kindergarten age! You may think your four-year-old is hard to keep up with, but that's because they're learning a lot of new skills very quickly over the course of this year.

DEVELOPMENTAL MILESTONES AT AGE 4

It seems like just yesterday that your baby was, truly, an infant. You might be sitting at the threshold of your child's fourth birthday wondering where all the time went. Most parents tend to be feeling now that their child really is starting to come into their own, and will miss a lot of the dependency their baby had on them. While your child was beginning to be independent, they're now much more realized — and need you much less. Or, at least, that's what it's going to feel like.

If your child has made great strides towards independence and has learned to complete certain tasks themselves, you did a great job, Dad. You've done all you needed to do in order to get your child behaviorally prepared for school, regardless of which schooling route you choose for your child. That being said, some children won't reliably perform the tasks you give them until they're around five-years-old. Watch out for that.

Your child should be able to speak fluently and be understood by strangers. They will process orally transmitted stories differently than they do the ones they read for themselves, as reading and listening process differently in the brain. Children who get read to out loud too often demonstrate an increased vocabulary than children whose caregivers often don't read to them.

Children will understand the use of pronouns at this point as well. They'll be able to memorize songs or poems, and may even recite them, an example of this is "Itsy Bitsy Spider." Your child will be able to recite longer, simpler stories. Perhaps, they'll even be making some of their own! They'll be able to name numbers and colors, understand the concepts of "same"-ness and "difference." You'll see your child start to copy capital letters, understand time, and draw people with arms and legs as opposed to sticks with heads!

Although your tot may be demonstrating quite a bit of independence at home, don't be fooled. They are likely very attached to you. While it may seem like they're ready to conquer the world, it's not uncommon for children to become incredibly upset at being separated from you — a fact you'll come to notice when your child goes to kindergarten, should you choose not to homeschool.

From here on, you'll want to be practicing your patience more than ever. Just because your tot is a bit older doesn't mean the no-yelling rules of the early years have gone away. Rather, you should expect from yourself that you can reason with your child. Your child is old enough to understand reason at basic levels, so there is no excuse to not use it as you teach your child the right types of behavior. This will also help foster more reasonable attitudes in your child for the future.

You will often find that behavior issues and anger can be talked through. Your four-year-old might be able to identify why they're upset. This will give you the chance to help your toddler process those feelings in healthier ways. You can teach your tot that it's okay to ask for breaks or time alone when they're upset. You should teach your child that it's even *okay* to be upset, as long as they talk about those feelings instead of acting out. Your toddler should understand that you two are part of a team when it comes to handling emotions, and that your tot can rely on you for guidance in their time of need. Dads, doing this well at this age will set the stage for you and your child's bond for the rest of their lives.

You can use timeouts, but be sure not to use them in ways that isolate your child. You should remain nearby. Even at four, children don't understand why they're being shut away — and this turns a time-out into a punishment, which is not the direction you want to go. This has cognitive implications for your child. When used appropriately, time-outs are a great way to introduce your child to the concept of de-escalating highly emotional situations. They can be a great way for your child to learn to wind down from their own tense feelings.

Physical exercise is another great way to teach your child to release any pent-up frustrations. Getting your child involved in organized sports will help your child expend all that extra energy they may have. There are likely many clubs and kids' teams locally that you can sign your child up for. If you want to teach your child a potentially life-saving skill at the same time, swimming lessons are a great idea (and you should probably do this anyway if you have the opportunity).

Advice For Parenting a Four-Year-Old

Four-year-olds pose a slew of additional challenges for parents, as the once pliant and accepting child begins to embrace a sense of defiance. There are going to be some moments of struggles between you and your child. You should expect to be challenged, and to stand firm by the rules and boundaries you've created (as long as they are reasonable).

Rules and boundaries help your child develop a sense of independence and identity. It's the first exposure your child will have to concepts of "right" and "wrong," and this understanding allows your child the ability to navigate social environments.

For that reason, you want to make extra sure you're praising good behavior and keeping your child on track with rules. You should encourage good behavior as much as you can, and really cement it into your child's brain that this behavior is the best behavior for them to have. To make the rules as easily accessible as possible, keep a simple chart of them on your fridge or in any other main area that your child has access to.

If you see that your child is particularly responsive to praise, you can reward them as well. Spice up the praise with a sticker. If your child collects enough stickers, reward them with a bigger prize — like a treat or a small toy.

Aside from rewards, you should encourage your child to participate in preparing meals with you. You should ensure that some of your meals are kid-friendly, meaning your child can feasibly do all parts of the making of the food by themselves. For instance, you could have your child pour cereal for everyone at breakfast. You should begin to teach your child some cooking skills that don't require a knife or a hot element.

Sometimes during these years, you're going to get angry and frustrated. It's important that you learn how to take a deep breath and step away from the situation so that it doesn't escalate any further. Remember, it's never okay to lose your temper with your child. But make sure, when you come back, that you're ready to solve the issue together with your child. And make sure you come back with some love and hugs.

SUPPORTING PRESCHOOLER
DEVELOPMENT (AGES 4-5)

Like with every stage leading up to now, play is important. However, its importance has evolved slightly. Instead of just helping your child become more cognitively aware of their surroundings, play is now important for your child's emotional expression. Preschoolers use play to convey feelings of joy, excitement, anger, or fear. They use play as a coping mechanism for negative emotions as well.

Where your child might've done a bunch of different things with play equally, they'll now start to have preferences for how they play. Maybe you have a child that dives headlong into sand or mud (rest in peace, washing machine), or maybe you have a child that likes to play pretend with dolls. Or perhaps they roleplay with other kids in games like House or Store, asserting that this pile of rocks is definitely food to be eaten. Whether your child is rough and tumble or they're more reserved, you should allow your child space to be able to play the way they want to safely.

Make sure that you allow your child to play on their own as well. You should make time for imaginative and creative play. Giving your child the chance to live in their own heads for a bit allows them to deepen their internal worlds, and you'll bear witness to the amazing things going on in your child's brain. Some types of play you can encourage towards this end are painting, drawing, or dress-up games. Music is another idea you could use — either with dancing and jumping around, or with taking up an actual instrument. An easy and cheap option towards this end is a recorder, which will help you gauge your child's interest without investing a ton of money and time.

At this age, strong inclinations towards activities become increasingly evident. You'll know now for sure whether you have an athlete, an artist, or a gamer on your hands. Perhaps, even, a little bookworm!

Keep reading to your preschooler. Read together, tell stories with one another, sing songs and recite nursery rhymes. Doing this has a twofold benefit to your child — you will be encouraging your child's speech development and talking, while simultaneously feeding their thinking and imagination.

Speaking of feeding, you'll want to continue cooking with your preschooler as well. You should get them interested in food, differentiating which food does what and what's healthy for them. At this time, your child will be able to grasp math concepts like "half," as well as measurements like "1 teaspoon." They should also understand time well enough that they understand what a half an hour is. You should teach them reasonable portion sizing, too.

Teaching your child these things early about food and cooking will help keep your child in healthy eating habits as they grow up. With your child able to cook for themselves, they will be less likely to want to order in — and will eat healthier foods as a result.

Your child should be able to use a plastic knife safely at this point. Of course, you should still oversee their use of a plastic knife — but it is good practice to start using one at this point. You can teach your child how to slice soft-cooked veggies, fruits, and cheese for themselves. Sandwiches are an easy meal to teach your child as well.

If your child doesn't show much interest in cooking, make it fun. You can invite your child's friend over for a cooking playdate!

You're riding on the tail end of the "mine" phase now, so it's important that you keep on top of your tot's possessive tendencies. Playing games with your child that encourage them to learn how to share and take turns with others is a great way to keep on top of this behavior. Sharing is still very difficult for your child to grasp as a concept — they will be worried that if they share, they won't be allowed to use the things again. You'll definitely want to praise that behavior when they do share, and a lot.

An example of how you can encourage this is by using building blocks together. While the two of you build the tower, say things like, "Now it's my turn to put a piece on the tower." You can alternate who's turn it is to put a piece on the tower that way. Additionally, you can swap blocks with one another by trading one color for another. If your child likes playing with dolls, you can say that you'll play with this doll, and then they can play with another. You can swap dolls back and forth as well. The important thing here is the exchange between you and your child. If there are other games you can do this with, they'll be just as good at teaching your tot this behavior.

KINDERGARTEN, PUBLIC SCHOOL, OR HOME SCHOOL?

Going to kindergarten is a huge step, both for you and your child. Whether you decide to home or public school, both of your schedules are about to shift to a more academic focus — which you'll maintain for much of the rest of your tot's development until adulthood. Kindergarten is essentially a daycare service designed to prepare your child for the first grade of elementary school, when delivered in a public school. At home, kindergarten shifts your usual focus of care to preparing your child for curriculum learning — whether you choose to do so at home or in a school setting.

Kindergarten is not necessary in many parts of the world, such as in some provinces in Canada and some states in the United States. In many places around the world, kindergarten is not federally mandated, but rather locally mandated. Before making the decision about whether or not to start kindergarten, you should check your local legislation requirements for pre-schooling your child. Your area may have different curricular requirements for kindergarten, or different credential requirements you must meet in order to teach your child at the kindergarten level. In most places, this typically means you'll need a bachelor's degree or an early childhood education diploma of some kind.

Your local legislation will also tell you at what age to begin kindergarten education. Many places in the world start kindergarten as young as two years of age, while others may wait as long as six or seven. Most countries tend to fall within the three to five year ranges, mostly at four years of age, to start kindergarten education.

Some parents choose not to enroll their children in kindergarten if given the choice by local legislature. These parents tend to make the argument that the schooling requirement age is too young for children to be separated for long periods of time from them, which is fair enough. Parents will use this time preparing their child as they see fit. It's not uncommon to hear of these parents encouraging their child to have more relaxed schedules as they ease their children into education, rather than jumping to full-day programs right away.

On the other hand, there are benefits to sending your children to kindergarten, even if it does seem early. For many parents, bringing children to kindergarten also means a return to working life — something that parents may come to be missing at this point if they've been off work to care for the kiddos at home.

At the end of the day, there are pros and cons to either option. You'll have to decide with your partner what is right for your family and especially your child. Without any ado, we will discuss the pros and cons of kindergarten in a public or home school setting so that you can make an informed decision.

The Case for Kindergarten at School

There are plenty of benefits a full-day kindergarten program has, though it can certainly feel like a scary next step for both you and your child. It's natural to be leery of letting your child go to full-day programs at this point.

Despite how scary it may be, your child can look forward to increased opportunities to develop their literacy and social skills at kindergarten. Being separated from you, your child will begin to understand themselves better, their self-conceptualization supported through distance from you. If the school you kindergarten with is the one you'll be sending your child for the rest of their elementary school career, this is a good opportunity for your child to grow a close bond with the school.

Kindergarten helps your child prepare for elementary school by developing the skills they'll need for first grade. They'll come to get used to a school setting and the schedule that goes with that, though from year to year the schedule shifts as your child develops. A kindergartener's schedule is somewhat different from a first-grader's, as your child becomes more able to focus for longer periods of time.

Kindergarten will also help to identify if your child has behavior or learning disabilities early on. In today's age, many parents go without testing their child out of a strong belief that their child is perfect. And, well, your child is perfect. Even if they have a learning disability. All that this knowledge will serve to provide you with is the tools to be able to work around these conditions in ways that will support your child's continued learning and independence. It will also assist your child in developing coping mechanisms to deal with their condition, rather than being plagued by feelings of confusion, otherness, and inadequacy that comes from not understanding why they may think differently than other kids.

There are benefits to a kindergarten program for you as well. If you have a hunger to return to work, full- or half-day kindergarten programs will afford you the time to be able to work without worrying about your child at home. Kindergartens provide your children with consistent, professional care, and you, the comfort of knowing that they are learning in a developmentally appropriate environment.

You will also be awarded the opportunity to have an active role in your child's formal education. Teachers and parents work together to teach their children, even in formal settings like schools.

The Case for Homeschooling Kindergarten

There are plenty of reasons why you may want to homeschool your children for kindergarten. No one will think less of you for it, especially seeing as kindergarten isn't even necessary in many parts of the world. It is true that kindergarten is focused more on getting your child ready for elementary school — skills you can certainly teach your child yourself, especially if you have a background in teaching. That said, you don't necessarily need experience as a teacher to teach kindergarten yourself.

The requirements you'll need to meet are going to be different per your location. Remember to check with your local legislature before you make the decision to homeschool. Without any further ado, let's make the case for homeschooling.

Rigidity in a schedule doesn't always fit well into yours or your child's lives — especially regarding the large time chunk that schooling requires. If you choose to homeschool, you'll have more flexibility with your time. You won't have to wake up early and rush out the door. Instead, you can have a more relaxed morning with your child. Taking your time waking up gives you a little extra quality snuggle time with your kid as well!

You won't have to worry about preparing lunch or getting your child dressed for the day. This can have the secondary effect of saving you some money. In some places of the world, foods that traditionally go into a child's lunch, like packaged snacks or sliced deli meats, often are more expensive than the foods you'd cook for meals.

Additionally, the stressors of driving on bad roads or in bad weather conditions are weeded out. If you live in a rural community, it's possible that your roads have seen better days and that the winters are treacherous for driving.

This flexibility is also helpful if ever your child is ill or something is preventing them from participating in their studies. While you should absolutely do your best to create a schedule and stick to the routine, at the very least, you can adjust it when you need to. With public schools, your only two options are for your child to be present, or they miss content. At homeschool, your child can miss a day, and maybe you just study on the weekend as well a little bit to catch up.

Medical reasons are another very large reason why parents can choose to homeschool. Children with severe allergies, chronic conditions, or certain disabilities may have more success in a homeschooling environment than in a public school setting. A homeschooling set up can help you tie in doctor or therapy appointments your children need into your routine without navigating around school bureaucracy.

While there are many school programs with exceptional services offered to children with special needs, at times, they are not enough to meet the needs of your children. You should keep this in mind as you weigh your options — perhaps you were interested in public schooling, but after seeing what their special services entail, it may not be a great fit after all. You may choose to go to another school, or if the schools that specialize in teaching kids with certain conditions are too far away, then you may decide you want to homeschool as well. Some schools are also more tolerant of independent education plans (IEPs) than others. Parents can choose not to homeschool just to weed out the difficulties of teaching an IEP to their children's teachers, or to avoid any kind of educational gatekeeping that may arise.

Or maybe you choose to homeschool because you want your child's curriculum to place more of an emphasis on the things public schools often leave out. Today, public schools often overlook the arts, the outdoors, important life skills (like how to do taxes), and physical education in favor of other subjects. Public schools, despite being a part of a community, also do not spend much time teaching your child how to be involved in the community with actions like volunteering or participating in any other community activities.

It's worth noting that homeschooling could also just simply be your preference. There's nothing wrong with that. As a father, maybe you'd rather be the person who teaches your child. Maybe you want to spend more time with them. There doesn't have to be a problem to navigate in order for you to choose homeschooling.

Whichever you choose to do, understand that both of your options have their pros and cons. It's up to you, your partner, and the needs of your child to decide which option is the best fit for your family. There is no shame in either course of action. Take your time to contemplate, and maybe ask your child's pediatrician for advice. You can also talk to your other parent friends, who may have valuable experience with kindergarten that you can use.

Things to Know for Homeschooling Kindergarten

After you've gone through the process of learning what your area's homeschooling requirements are, you should then do some research regarding the different curricula options available to you. Choosing a curriculum for your child is one of the many benefits of homeschooling, on top of being able to tailor existing curricula to your needs. To give an example, you could design a curriculum for math lessons that are adjusted to your child should they struggle with numeracy. One of the ways you can do this is to incorporate math into storytelling or music, or to teach math processes to completion rather than having to review those concepts repeatedly (as your child would have to do in public schools).

Interest-led learning is another option available to you. Allowing your child's interests to dictate the learning process is a great way to keep them engaged with their learning. This may involve field trips, research, projects, and so on. All this just by helping your child pursue specific interests.

Basically, any curriculum at a public school can be taught at a home school but more personalized. Kindergarten teaches your child math, language, scientific, artistic, and physical skills. You should focus on reading and writing, crafts, and games to keep your child engaged. You can also add other subjects into the mix as they suit you and your child, like social sciences, music, or a second language.

Whichever type of curriculum you decide upon, you should set goals for your child and develop a routine. Having a schedule and reinforcing the schedule early on sets your child up for success later down the line when time management and organization skills are absolutely necessary. School routine has the added benefit of preparing your child for a working environment as well. It'll also help you keep on schedule, too — especially if you go through the effort of creating lesson plans.

Regarding goal-setting, you should endeavor to create reasonably achievable objectives for your child. This may look like a certain grade, or reading a certain amount every week, so on.

You should go out of your way to incorporate fun into your curriculum. Children learn best through fun because they'll be far more engaged if they're having fun than if they're bored!

Take your time to develop your style of teaching and to figure out what works for you and your kid.

Developing a Kindergartener's Reading List

The best books for your kindergartener are ones that are fun but teach lessons about life as well. You should take care to pick books that feature lovable and diverse characters, with heartwarming themes, and new vocabulary.

There are some beloved classics of children's literature, like *Clifford* and *The Cat in the Hat.* Many parents will default to the books they read in their own childhood, though this may not always be the best way to go about developing your reading list. Since you were a child, the world has changed! Recent books will be more likely to address the issues and lessons relevant to the current social climate, so you should focus on those types of books if you can. With that said, Dr. Seuss's work is timeless fun and there's nothing wrong with having some of his works in your collection — as long as you have other books as well.

Reading lists exist all over the internet, or you can go out to a bookstore with your kid. If you peruse the selections together, your child may point out the books they're most interested in. This method will help keep your child interested in reading and caring for the books they receive.

6

WHAT TO EXPECT NEXT

*Y*our journey through early childhood is nearing its midpoint. Your child is nearly past the pre-operational stage of their development, gradually entering into the new challenges of the pre-schooling and grade schooling age. Though many of the struggles of the early years may persist until after five years of age, this is normal — all children develop differently.

You can expect from this point that the struggles of the early years will slowly diminish as your child's understanding of the world matures. Your child is growing rapidly and beginning to refine their gross and fine motor skills. Your child will have likely grown a vocabulary of around 1,500 words. They should be speaking in sentences of five to seven words.

Symbolic understanding of the world will continue to develop all the way through till about seven years of age, and from there, that development will slow. This means that symbolic play (like riding a broom and pretending it's a horse) and manipulating symbols will slowly recede.

Your child has not yet developed a concrete understanding of logic. It will come in the years following the pre-operational stage, so be sure to keep using your reason with your child so that they can pick up on your discriminating thought processes.

There are many important lessons for you to teach your child going forward. In order to raise a confident, kind, and successful child, it takes more than just being present.

RAISING A CONFIDENT CHILD

It's no secret that the key to your child's well-being and success as an adult is their self-esteem. It's important to set a precedent for parenting success from day one with your child in this regard. To raise a confident child, a father needs to embody all the qualities he wants to impart upon his child. He needs to treat his child with kindness, and give the space his child needs to thrive and be their own person.

Anything less than that can result in some issues in the future. Poor self-esteem and self-image issues often lead to behavior problems, like bullying, acting out, and so on. Your child will lash out due to their insecurities, and won't have the resources to properly cope with their feelings.

Where it comes to helping your child develop good self-esteem, there are a few things that you need to keep in mind and do as your child grows. The first thing to keep in mind, Dads, is your responsiveness.

As men, we have a tendency to not express our positive feelings as much. It's time to do away with that way of thinking — it's not good for us, and it's not good for our children. In the pursuit of boosting our children's self-esteem, we should be the loudest people in the room cheering for our children's successes. You must be your child's biggest fan, their stay-at-home cheerleader, the veritable king of patting backs. Every time your child does something good, cheer for them to make them feel good about themselves.

Take note that this doesn't mean over-praising. Over-praising is giving praise for things that don't necessarily require praise. Doing this lowers the bar, so to speak, of praiseworthy activities and takes away the dopamine hit from doing some truly remarkable. It also makes your child less inclined to push themselves to try harder. To navigate this, it's a great idea to praise hard work and determination.

This is only one of the ways you can boost self-esteem, of course. Sometimes it might even be better to know when stepping back is more important than stepping up. Letting your child take risks, make choices, and solve problems will all contribute to their growing self-esteem. Encouraging your child to stick with the things they start will be your job. If they fail, you can help put them back on the path they chose. Whatever you do, don't shame your child and keep urging them not to give up on themselves. Your belief in your child helps them to believe in themselves.

You should give your child space to explore their interests as well. Let them do the things they show interest in, and make sure they follow that through to completion. It doesn't necessarily matter what these tasks are. It can be anything from running a lap to beating a few levels in a video game. The key to this is that they finish what they start.

Where it comes to your child's self-value, things can go wrong at the infancy stage. Responsiveness during infancy sets the tone for your child's self-esteem for the future. Parenting styles that have an increased amount of touch help children develop self-worth — on average, high-touch parenting styles lead to more secure children.

Babies who came into the world with more needs than others are at higher risk of receiving negative responses. Parents can sometimes feel overwhelmed by the intense demands of their infants, which can impact the attachment bonds between parent and child. Attachment produces mutual sensitivity between parents and babies; this relationship often predicts your child's future behaviors. Insecurely attached children are more likely to have behavioral issues in school, for instance. Securely attached, children will go on to be more confident in taking risks and trying new things.

How to Raise Confidence

It's never too late to start building new habits that will help you raise a confident child. Not every mistake you've made during the parenting phase is irreparable, so don't be hard on yourself or hold yourself to unrealistic standards of perfection. In fact, making mistakes and gracefully correcting them is one of the things you should teach your child to learn to do.

There's a lot of work that all parents need to put into themselves to be able to teach the valuable lessons required for a self-confident child. Largely, this is because many people go without feeling secure themselves. Parents have to work through years of reinforced beliefs in themselves and in the world in order to support their child's positive perspectives in both regards later on.

Your first step will be to heal the wounds you feel from your past. Some people are plagued more than others by their memories or mental health. If this isn't you, feel free to move on. However, if you have any concern whatsoever, you need to know that it is okay to seek outside guidance for those issues. You're no less for seeking help. In fact, you're much stronger for it. If you're prepared to work on yourself, but you're not ready to seek help just yet, take baby steps.

If you're concerned about how your actions will impact your child, look to your parents, or to any of the adult influences you've had in your life. List some of the specific things your parents did to build your self-image. And then think about some of the negative feelings your parents had that affected you. Your child will be likewise impacted by those exact things.

A parent's unhappiness transfers to their children. This happens so naturally that fetuses can sense and feel their mother's emotions and actually respond to them. When mom's not feeling well, neither is the baby. Now that your child is born, they're going to pick up on both you and your partner's emotions. To you, it'll be like you're looking into a mirror. To them, it'll be the same. Make sure that the image the both of you project to one another is one of kindness and love, especially towards yourself.

Spending extra time with your child, especially playtime, is another way to help your child raise their confidence. Spending all this time basically tells your child that they are worth your time, and that they are valuable to you. These feelings of importance and accomplishment stem directly from winning your attention, so be sure to give your child your sole attention with play.

Your children will know when your attention is on them or not. Kids may not be as developed as you are, but they're clever and highly empathetic. If you're thinking about work, and you're not completely present with your child, they will sense that.

Don't allow yourself to be distracted by anything outside of your child when you're playing together. You need the play time as much as your child does. Play puts you at the same level as your child, helping you assume the perspective and understanding your child has towards the world. It's an incredible opportunity to bond, and learn more about the little person you've been raising all this time.

The interest you pay in your child now directly correlates with how much interest your child will show in you later. If you do things with your baby early on, they'll be more willing to do things with you as they grow. You'll become their go-to person.

You'll know you've done a good job raising a secure child when they address their peers and adults by their names or titles. Children who use names open doors for themselves with other people, break barriers between them and the world. It even has the ability to soften corrective discipline.

Discipline plays into self-esteem by way of how it's used to create a schedule, and develop determination. If you encourage your child to work at their special talents, and help them build on them, they will develop self-confidence as a result of this hard work. Regardless of what your tot loves to do, support them every step of the way. Don't expect them to be talented in all the ways that you might be, but let them come to you to tell you what *they* feel they're talented at. Chances are, your child will work harder at the things they want to do rather than the things they may simply be naturally talented at.

By doing this, you'll be able to watch your child absolutely blossom. Without being expected to excel at the things they don't care about, and given the room to do the things they love, you'll be raising an individual who prides themselves on the things they can achieve.

Your children are too valuable to be left to chance. Don't let whatever happens happen. You should approach every aspect of your child's development with a flexible plan that adjusts only to suit the needs, wants, and personality of your child.

You should consider this with regards to who your child makes friends with as well. You'll want to screen everyone who becomes a person of importance in your child's life — their friends, their coaches, their teachers. You should put a keen eye on anyone who has any type of authority or sway in your child's life. Watch out for your child's signals — whether they feel calm or upset by the interaction they'd just had with someone else. You really want to stay on top of this because your child's self-confidence will be impacted by everyone they meet, not just by you or your partner.

To do this, you can turn your house into the main point of contact between your child and other children. You should ensure that your household is inviting to your child's friends, and their parents as well, so that you can keep a close eye on them. Hosting the neighborhood, so to speak, allows you to track your child and their feelings throughout the interaction.

You might also consider giving your child a "wall of fame," so to speak. Maybe have a cabinet, some shelf space, or some specifically allotted refrigerator real estate for your child's awards and drawings. Keep pictures of them with you in those places. Decorate your home with images of the love your family shares, and memories of all the things you have done together.

Keeping these around throughout your child's life is very important. Your child's sense of self and their confidence comes from you and the home you've made. The nurturing of their caregivers and the love of the people in their life are the components needed to raising a confident, self-loving child.

TEACHING KINDNESS

Kindness is a learned behavior, just like all others. Parents have to embody and use kindness in their daily lives if they wish to teach that to their children. Often, parents will even have to work harder to show they value kindness and helping others as much as they value a child's performance in school. It is, however, important that you *do* put the effort in to show you value kindness.

When you expect your child to act kindly, you should do so as well. Your child will pick up on your behaviors. All that you do are things that your child will eventually do themselves. So, if you are persistently kind in front of your child, your child will grow to be a kind person as well.

There's some evidence to suggest that children are "hardwired" to become kind, as a result of our empathetic nature. Due to our evolutionary biology, humans are incredibly empathetic to one another — the pains of the group affect us as individuals profoundly. Empathy is the key to kindness, so one can say that kindness is essentially part of our nature. However, not every child falls in line with this or understands kindness and empathy in the same way others do. It's possible that your definition of kindness differs from that of people from other cultures and societies, or even other people within your culture groups.

By rewarding small acts of kindness, you will be setting up your child with the best chance at growing up as kind as you can. You don't want to go overboard, though. One of the most important lessons you'll ever teach your child is that kindness is its own reward — you should not expect anything in return for being kind, you simply should be kind.

And with that said, you should also teach your child that kindness has its limits. Selflessness sounds like a great trait in theory, but it often comes at the expense of the child feeling like they're simply not worth the selfishness. You need to teach your child the boundaries there are to kindness and how they differ between people, all the while affirming your child's self-worth and confidence.

One of the best ways you can teach your child empathy and kindness is to have them interact with people from different backgrounds. The key to your child learning empathy is to learn that there are as many perspectives in the world as there are people. Exposing your child to as many different ways of thinking and living is the number one way to raise an empathetic individual.

Setting A Positive Example

The more good deeds you practice in front of your child, the more they will begin to mimic those deeds. While your child may not be able to make heads or tails of why you're doing the things you're doing, what they will come to understand is the consequences for those actions. When your child sees you leaving behind smiles and good memories in the places you go, they will come to understand the reward one receives for being a kind individual.

When it comes to exhibiting kindness in front of your child, a little goes a long way. You could hold open the door for strangers, drop change into tip jars, let someone go in front of you. Greeting people who pass you by with a short hello or even a smile is great.

When there's someone in need around you, help them. Send out messages or phone calls to people who you know are having a rough time to check on them, practice sensitivity in the home with your partner, child, and any other family member. If you have the funds, pay it forward to strangers — maybe you pay for someone's order in the drive thru lane. Donate old books, games, and clothes to those who are in need.

As soon as schooling age comes along, you could send your kid into school with some cookies to give to people. You and your kid could even bake those yourselves!

Or maybe do a service for your neighbors. Cutting grass or doing a little weeding for them, shoveling snow in the winter, or raking up leaves are a great way to show kindness to your community.

Let your child see and hear you compliment people genuinely. It's a shame people feel so uncomfortable to boost one another up in today's environment — and everyone likes a compliment every now and then. Take the time to notice other peoples' skills and point them out to encourage your child to do the same. This has the double effect of showing your child that you value others' efforts, which may help them learn to value their own.

Think about the things that you would like for someone to do for you, or that would make your life easier. That's the type of behavior you want your child to learn from you. Your acts of kindness don't need to be huge, but if you treat others the way you want to be treated, even small efforts go a long way.

Living this way has the added benefit of improving your mental health as well, Dad. Showing kindness and doing things that make others grateful markedly increases one's self-image — the influx of dopamine that comes from doing something well for someone else sees to that. Don't be afraid to show and practice kindness wherever you go. You'll feel better for it, and your child will grow up kinder for it as well.

Take Your Own Advice

All the things you do, all the things you say, make lasting impressions on your child. The things you say to yourself and about the world around you will color the way your child views the world and themselves for the rest of their lives.

You can't expect that all the lessons you're trying to teach your child will take root if you don't live them yourself. So, here are the ten greatest things you should keep in mind as you parent and go through life with your family:

1. Become the best version of yourself.
   Unhappy people raise unhappy children, this is just a fact. You need to navigate the things about yourself that you don't necessarily like and change to become someone you love, or learn to love yourself. Preferably both. This looks different for everyone, and it's a never-ending process of reflection to action. Just know that you are always capable of changing, you're never too old to be a better person.

2. Celebrate with your whole family as often as possible. Individual victories should be celebrated together — your family lives and breathes by the strength of each of its

members. Since everyone has such a profound impact on one another, everybody should celebrate everyone else's victories. Additionally, your holidays and so forth should be communally celebrated as well.

3. Prioritize your marriage over your children. You need to make sure you're paying attention and respect to your partner, and vice versa. Happy marriages and partnerships lead to happier children, and happier parents. Go out of your way to compliment your partner, and make time for date nights.

4. When your tot talks to you, be sure to give them your undivided attention. Put down your phone or your book, and turn your body so that you're fully facing your child. This is a strategy in active listening that makes all communication run smoother and more positively. It will go a long way to improving your child's sense of self-value, and being present in the moment with your child will improve your bond.

5. Eat regular meals together as a family, like dinner. Your partner's work schedules (and your own) may end up changing when your

family eats together. However, you should make sure that you do at some point at least once a day. While dinner is the most common meal to eat with family, it could also be breakfast or lunch.

6. Teach yourself to manage your emotions, and teach your child how to do so as well. Creating a system of coping mechanisms to help support you and your child through tough times is a good idea — and they'll help you through those situations without accidentally lashing out at someone who didn't deserve it.

7. Build meaningful relationships, so you can teach your children how to build them as well. Your child should see you foster your bonds with others outside of your family — friendships, neighborly relationships, and so on. Your child will learn how to treat other people based on how you treat the people around you.

8. Set reasonable boundaries for you and your children. Your child should know that you won't go invading their privacy, and you should expect the same from them.

Compromise often with your child to find solutions to sticky situations.

9. Get as much sleep as you can, and ensure that your children get enough sleep too. This bears really no need for explanation other than sleep is incredibly healthy, and the two of you should see you're getting enough of it.

10. The journey is more important than its conclusion. Focus more on the adventures you and your child will have, rather than the lessons that come out of them.

RAISING A SUCCESSFUL CHILD

The secret to raising successful children is, in fact, not really much of a secret at all. It's clear to see that the relationship parents have with their children has direct effects on their children's happiness and success in the future.

"Duh," you might say. And, yeah. Admittedly, this is certainly not a surprise to hear. Perhaps it's even stating the obvious.

You probably don't need a scientist to be able to tell you that, but if you do, there are several published studies and books that you can read (including this one) that stand behind this truth.

Children who are raised feeling accepted for who they are and nurtured to be the best they can possibly be, will have the best chances of success in adulthood. They'll also have markedly improved well-being and life satisfaction when compared to someone who unfortunately did not have those things. This goes back to attachment, and establishing a secure attachment with your child.

Securely attached children are ones who develop a wealth of confidence and tend to have a more positive outlook on the world. By cultivating a close parent-child relationship through being warm, responsive, and engaged, you are sure to raise a child who strives for success.

Success, however, is no simple thing to define. So let's explore what success is, what it means, and the mindset to develop success both in yourself and your children.

The Subjectivity of Success

On the internet, there's about fifteen different articles on the front page of Google that talk about how to raise a successful child. Some of the tips are even helpful, but they often miss the mark. It's all well and fine to discuss parenting methods, but there's really no metric to success. Success is subjective.

Your metric for success may even be different from your partner's. Almost always, it will be different from your child's. While success is something that you have to define yourself, you shouldn't stick to it like it's gospel. You should get to know your opinions regarding success early on, and adjust them as your child grows.

People often put too high or low their expectations to call something successful. In truth, the only person you'll be hurting by doing either is yourself. This is a good life lesson to teach your child, but one few parents take to heart as they raise their child.

Many parents have dreams for their children. This is no surprise. It is often heard that children grew up with expectations from their parents that they'd go to law school, or become a doctor, what have you. Parents will put their children through years of training in sports the child wasn't even interested in, all to say that their child would be an Olympian.

To some people, success isn't defined by how much money they make or achieving dreamy accomplishments. It's okay if one's metric for success is simply doing what they love to do. Maybe your metric of success is providing the best possible upbringing for your child that you can.

Therefore, there's no catch-all way to be successful or to raise successful children. It's simply not possible to create when there can be as many definitions for success as there are people in this world.

The world's most successful people understand this for themselves as well. While successful people tend to share a few habits, they relate more to their mindsets, their goals, and the quality of their self-care. Successful people define for themselves what success is and commit to personal growth. They practice regular self-care routines, and conduct themselves strategically in order to reach their goals — whatever those may be.

As you raise your child, you should embody the mindset of a successful person. Though you may not initially feel like you're a successful person, the process that successful people go through to improve themselves will make you feel like you are.

That's the whole point of it, and the secret to where successful people find stores of energy to be able to do great things.

Instead of having rigid definitions of success, allow your child to construct what success for them would mean for both of you. Set short-term goals that your child can aspire to in the meantime, and let them tell you what their dreams for the future are. Or, foster the things that they love to do. If you have a little artist on your hands, you should encourage them to keep doing art rather than discourage them from what they love.

You cannot be successful in life if you aren't happy. Even if the financial situation is sound, a person will not feel accomplished in their lives if they feel like they're not doing the things that they believe they're meant to be doing. You should consider this for yourself — have you personally ever felt accomplished doing something you had no passion to do? Probably not. More on that point, have you ever felt accomplished doing something you had to do because of an overwhelming expectation to do so?

The chances are, no. Probably not.

To support your child's success, allow them to define what success means for them. Of course, there's nothing wrong with challenging your child to strive for greater things — and you absolutely should. But you should make sure those challenges fall in line with the things they love to do and the things they need to do for themselves. By doing this, you'll be encouraging good habits of goal-setting and self-care that helped the most successful people in the world get established.

Goal-Setting

Many people go through life without a strategy regarding goal-setting. You'll hear many people talk about how they wanted to do something huge and awesome for themselves, but don't actually have a plan to get there in the first place. This is relatively common. They don't teach realistic goal-setting in schools, after all.

It's good to have dreams. A dream gives you the space to develop a framework for success — the journey to the end of the road, so to speak.

It may be too early at this point for your child to have a definable dream, let alone one that doesn't change from week to week as children explore their personalities. However, it's never too early to understand how to develop smart goals and teach your child how to do so as well.

Smart goals are ones that are realistic and attainable in a predefined portion of time, which serve to get you one step closer to your dream goal. You can think about it like you're breaking down your dreams into a series of checkpoints. A list of prerequisites to fill before you can get the overarching achievement.

These goals are ones that are specific and measurable as well. You would define the thing that you want to be able to do at that time, and the metric for whether you did that or not. For your child, an example of this type of goal would be getting an A on their upcoming test. The goal is specific, and you've outlined the parameter for its success.

The next important thing is that it is, in fact, achievable. But not just achievable at any point. It should be time bound, and relevant to the things that are happening in your life right now. Basically, this just means that these are things you can do for yourself in the short term. For instance, if your goal is to get more active with your kid, then maybe one of your smaller goals is to go out for a ten-minute walk every few hours.

It's important to set goals responsibly and kindly. There's nothing to be gained from unrealistic goals with no plan to see them through — this will just lead to feelings of frustration and getting overwhelmed. In life, no one skips the line. It takes hard work to achieve one's dreams, and the process of hard work can be grueling if it's not broken down at least a little bit.

Breaking down those goals has the added benefit of making you feel like you are accomplishing something, even if you haven't achieved the dream quite yet. This has the effect of releasing dopamine (the happy feel-good drug) in the brain, which will encourage you to keep doing the things you're doing. Keeping this in mind, you'll be able to set goals for yourself that keep you motivated, and you'll be able to teach your child how to do so as well.

Teach, Guide, but Don't Control

Throughout this book, we've discussed at length the importance of allowing your child to dictate the flow of learning and development. When it comes to success, you'll be keeping with this formula.

Without being a disengaged parent, you want to give your children the space to be independent and to achieve things on their own. You should give your children things that they can own and control. For instance, their toys and the things in their room. By teaching them to clean up after themselves and to take care of the things that they own, your child will share the responsibility of their care with you.

That isn't to say that you abandon your child. Your child is far too young to be caring for themselves in every way. They will need their fathers to help guide them and encourage them through the trials of life that are sure to come their way.

Rather, you should embrace the concept of allowing your children to hold some say in their upbringing. Allow your child's interests and goals to dictate the way that you support them and encourage them. This will also help you analyze where your child may need more encouragement; cleaning one's room is never the *fun* thing to do, but your child will still need to learn to do things for themselves!

This has the added benefit of demonstrating to your child that you value them as people. Embracing their individuality helps them feel more confident doing the things they love and exploring who they are as people. With dad on their side, children feel empowered to learn who they are, what they love, and so on. While this journey may lead to a lot of heartbreak for your child, this is an important part of life, and you can't expect to shield your baby from hurt forever.

This is why it's important to support your child with encouragement rather than doing everything for them. You can fill in your child's needs for things that they can't do for themselves while simultaneously empowering them to learn the skills to be able to do so — that is the job of a parent, after all.

As it's an impossible task to expect that you can protect your child from life, you should not place your focus on raising a happy kid. Now, you might read this and cringe — of course, you should do your best to make every experience with your child a positive one. That said, for the times when something comes your child's way that is a hurtful experience, they need to be armed with the emotional and mental tools to be able to cope.

There will come times where your child will come home from school or work with terrible news, and it's important not to shame them during those difficult times. Instead, you should encourage them to keep trying.

Your focus while raising your tot should be to develop them into productive and moral individuals. You should focus on praising their hard work and their conviction rather than the grade they received. A child is benefited more by being praised for their efforts, rather than their accomplishment. This also means that you should be praising them more often.

Ideally, you should see that your child is working hard at something and praise them all throughout that process. At the end, when they're awarded with the accomplishment all that hard work has turned up, then you can tell them things like, "I knew you could do it, you worked so hard." Or something else to that effect. This reinforces the idea that determination and hard work is king where it comes to success — which it is.

These are all things to keep in mind as your child grows. Think of them as habits and mindsets for you to establish during the early years, which you'll keep all throughout your child's life. Better yet, adopt these mindsets for every person in your life — including yourself. Not only is setting a positive example the best way to impart good life skills and mentalities on your children, but it's also important for *your* sake.

For now, you should focus on teaching your kids to help out around the house without being asked. That's going to be your biggest task at these early ages! You wanted to start small and then work your way up to the more complicated tasks that will come with age and new life situations.

If there's one thing to take from this book, it's that everything matters. Especially the little things. Your children are incredibly impressionable in early childhood. So impressionable in fact that a simple throwaway comment can have effects that last a lifetime. Be mindful of all that you do and say, and make sure that everything is purposeful.

SUPPORTING YOUR PARTNER

Whether you are the primary caregiver or the secondary caregiver, you have the responsibility as a father to support the people in your life who play a role in raising your child. While everyone's circumstances are different, the chances are you're probably getting some help from your family, the child's mother, your partner, or perhaps even your friends and community in the raising of your children. Or, at least, you should seek that support.

Becoming a parent has certainly been the most life-changing experience for you, and for the people you live with — most definitely for your child's mother and your partner as well. Dads have to be there for their partners in order to keep the quality of your combined parenting as high as possible.

Remember, you are a team where it comes to raising your children. Here are some key ways you can be there for the people who help you bring up your kid:

1. Encourage them in their roles. Whether they're a new mother, a new father, a step-parent, or a friend or family member who's taking an active role in raising your child,

make sure you express your gratitude to them and assure them whenever possible. Raising children is tough and daunting, and it's easy for anyone to feel like they're a half step away from messing up drastically. This anxiety is best eased by your gentle encouragement and support.

2. Be warm. Your caring attitude should extend to everyone in your life, not just your child. You should seek to nurture everyone in your life, empowering them to be their best selves through your example. Love the people you surround yourself with, and the people who surround your children the most.

3. Stay informed and pitch in. You'll want to be involved in the decisions being made for your children, and it's more than likely that there will be several discussions that pop up through your child's life that the two of you will disagree on. Be willing to listen, and expect to be listened to in turn — doing this, you and your partner should be able to make some compromises or even find better solutions!

4. Take turns. You're going to need a break, and so will your partner. Make sure that the

division of work with raising a child is equal, and that both of you are well rested so that you can give it your best at every moment.

5. Make time for yourselves. Regardless of if you're in a romantic relationship with your child's other caregiver, you should make time to foster the relationship you have with them regardless. Make plans to spend time with them child-free from time to time. Strengthen your bonds! This will be good for unifying you as well as for keeping up your mental health, as it is easy to forget that you're also a fun-needing person while taking on all the duties of being a father.

AFTERWORD

So, dads, this is it.

With this, you've learned all there is to know about the fundamentals of raising your toddler. From age one to four, we've gone over all the most common issues surrounding early childhood development. You've got all the tools, and it's time to put them into perspective.

Right from the first chapter, you learned about the developmental milestones that would be coming your way and how to navigate them. You've got a handle on how to potty-train, how to childproof your home, what your children need to eat, and so much more. We've discussed parenting, positive psychological methods of parenting, the kindergarten question, and even how to raise confident, kind, and successful children.

You're armed, dads. The purpose of this book was to supply you with a wealth of knowledge from one father to another about how to raise a child. As fathers, we don't have a wealth of information at our disposal about what our role is as a parent. For many of us, it kind of feels like we're meant to be left flailing while the baby's mother takes over all the nurturing aspects of parenting. This is unfair, as father's deserve a share in the task of caring for their children and developing close relationships with their tots.

Mothers are often the ones opening up their hearts and becoming vulnerable for the sake of their children, fully embodying the experience of motherhood. Fathers are usually left to the sidelines as supporting characters, rather than active protagonists in their children's lives. Dads, don't be afraid to assert yourself. Let those walls come crumbling down and embrace the sensitivity and love a father needs to raise their children well. Share in all the aspects of parenting now because before you know it, those opportunities will be gone.

Children don't stay children for long. When you're waving goodbye to your child as they walk to the doors of their grade one classroom, you'll wonder where the last six years have gone. Sometimes you'll be left wondering when they got so tall. Or when they got so smart.

It's important that you take the time to be hands-on during these formative years, or you'll miss them entirely. There's no worse feeling than learning that your child just accomplished something big, and you weren't there to be a part of it. Those moments come fast, and they leave at the same speed they came. Before you know it, your child's a teenager, and you have to deal with much more *complicated* and *life-ruining* (as stated by your child) challenges, leaving you hungry for the days when your child's needs were simpler, to say the least.

Being a hands-on dad as someone who's never been a father before is a daunting task with lots of twists and turns. There's no simple path forward as a father. Parenting is tricky, and what's more, it's stressful. No parent can say that they didn't worry about raising their children, that they didn't have any concerns whatsoever. Even the most confident of people are riddled with nervousness when they think of their children, asking themselves all the "what ifs" they could possibly think of.

This isn't necessarily a bad thing. In fact, it could be argued that the existence of those fears is one of the makes of a truly good parent. That you have concern at all shows that you deeply care about doing a good job for your kid. We all look to parenting while we discuss who we are, and most importantly, where we fall short. You yourself may have thought that you'd wished your parents would've done something different while raising you. You should take those thoughts to heart as you're raising your first child.

There's no amount of literature that's going to make you into the perfect parent. The truth of the matter is, perfect parenting doesn't exist. It can't, even. Perfection isn't real, and it's certainly not a realistic goal to aspire to. Especially where it comes to parenting — perfectionism isn't helpful.

Instead, what you should aspire to be is your best. Every day should be met with a conviction to conquer fatherhood's challenges, personal feelings, and create a habit of growth. You should seek to develop your internal world as much as you develop your children's external world. Wrangle your inner demons, navigate your concerns and your sensitivities, and make every moment about being with your child and being the best man you can possibly be. It's this mindset that makes a man into a good father, one that their children aren't afraid to lean on and talk to in their times of need.

No one became good at anything without making a few mistakes. You should expect to make them, even though you're trying everything in order to keep from doing so. Every child is different, there are few universal truths about parenting. Much of our information about parenting is based on what tends to happen *on average*, but your child is most likely not average.

You'll have to learn how to be flexible with your routine and your plans, as well as with yourself. Forgive yourself for the small errors you make, and instead, focus on what you did to put things right. By doing this, you'll be providing your child with a great example of what healthy self-growth looks like. But moreover, you'll be adopting a mindset for yourself that will change your life for the better.

Get excited, dads. Your life is about to become a lot more dynamic and interesting than you ever thought it'd be. While you embrace the qualities of the role models you hold dear, make sure you're honing your routine and adjusting it as the years pass by. Learn to let loose during playtime and return to the time when you had a more happy-go-lucky mindset yourself. Be discriminating with the parenting advice you receive, and don't be tricked by the myths many parents are duped to believe. Enjoy your time, and most importantly, fill up your heart with cherishable moments.

Love your children and love them hard. Hold your children and give them plenty of snuggles and kisses. A dad's love is incredibly powerful, sending messages to children that words can't always convey.

REFERENCES

Baruch, G. K., & Barnett, R. C. (1981). *Fathers' participation in the care of their preschool children.* Sex Roles *7,* 1043-1055. https://link.springer.com/article/10.1007/BF00288505

Ben-Joseph, E. P. (n.d.). *Nutrition guide for toddlers.* KidsHealth from Nemours. https://kidshealth.org/en/parents/toddler-food.html

Christiansen, K. T. (n.d.). *How to homeschool kindergarten.* Kindergarten Connection. https://thekindergartenconnection.com/how-to-homeschool-kindergarten/

de Bellefonds, C. (2019). *Dressing skills: Teaching your child how to dress herself.* What To Expect. https://

www.whattoexpect.com/toddler/photo-gallery/
dressing-skills.aspx

Ginsburg, K. R. (2007). *The importance of play in promoting healthy child development and maintaining strong parent-child bonds.* Pediatrics Official Journal of the American Academy of Pediatrics 119(1) 182-191. doi: https://doi.org/10.1542/peds.2006-2697

Gottman, J. M. (1997). *Raising an emotionally intelligent child.* Simon Schuster.

Kelmon, J. (2016). *When should kids start kindergarten?* Great! Schools. https://www.greatschools.org/gk/articles/redshirting-kindergarten/

Krisch, J. A. (2021). *The science of dad and the 'father effect.'* Fatherly. https://www.fatherly.com/health-science/science-benefits-of-fatherhood-dads-father-effect/

Lamb, M. E. (1976). *The role of the father in child development.* John Wiley & Sons, Inc. Hoboken, New Jersey, United States.

Lonczak, H. S. (2021). *What is positive parenting? A look at the research and benefits.* Positive Psychology. https://positivepsychology.com/positive-parenting/

Masters, M. (2021). *How much should a toddler eat?* What To Expect. https://www.whattoexpect.com/toddler-nutrition/toddler-eating-enough.aspx

Mazel, S. (2018). *First steps.* What To Expect. https://www.whattoexpect.com/first-year/first-steps/

Murkoff, H. & the What To Expect editorial team. (2019). *Behavior and discipline.* What To Expect. https://www.whattoexpect.com/toddler-behavior-and-discipline-tips.aspx

Murkoff, H. & the What To Expect editorial team. (2019). *Best shoes for toddlers: A buying guide.* What To Expect. https://www.whattoexpect.com/toddler/toddler-gear/best-shoes-for-toddlers.aspx

Murkoff, H. & the What To Expect editorial team. (2019). *How to help your toddler make friends.* What To Expect. https://www.whattoexpect.com/toddler/how-to-help-your-toddler-make-friends.aspx

Murkoff, H. & the What To Expect editorial team. (2019). *Tips for outings for kids.* What To Expect. https://www.whattoexpect.com/toddler/kids-day-out/tips-for-outings-for-kids.aspx

O'Connor, A. (2018). *Potty training tips for boys and girls.* What To Expect. https://www.whattoexpect. com/toddler-development/potty-training.aspx

O'Connor, A. (2018). *Signs your toddler is ready to be potty trained.* What To Expect. https://www. whattoexpect.com/toddler/potty-training/signs-of-readiness.aspx

Paris, J., Beeve, K., & Springer, C. (2019). *Introduction to curriculum for early childhood education.* College of the Canyons.

Pediatric Associates of Franklin. (n.d.). *The importance of a father in a child's life.* Pediatric Associates of Franklin. https://www. pediatricsoffranklin.com/resources-and-education/ pediatric-care/the-importance-of-a-father-in-a-childs-life/

Taylor, M. (2021). *Your toddler's feeding schedule.* What To Expect. https://www.whattoexpect.com/toddler/ eating-and-nutrition/sample-toddler-feeding-schedule

The Bump Editors. (2017). *Baby proofing checklist: Before baby comes home.* The Bump. https://www. thebump.com/a/checklist-babyproofing-part-1

The What To Expect editorial team. (2019). *Best toys for toddlers.* What To Expect. https://www. whattoexpect.com/toddler/photo-gallery/best-toys-for-toddlers.aspx#1

Valenzuela, J. P. (2021). *How to measure your kids' foot - 2 Simple steps to determine foot length and foot width.* Fitting Children's Shoes. https:// fittingchildrenshoes.com/how-to-measure-your-kids-foot-2-simple-steps-to-determine-foot-length-and-foot-width

Printed in Great Britain
by Amazon